CAREER EDUCATION

A READER

Edited by

David C. Wigglesworth
President
TRA Technical Research Associates, Inc.

Canfield Press
San Francisco
A Department of Harper & Row, Publishers, Inc.
New York • Evanston • London

CAREER EDUCATION, First edition. Copyright © 1975 by David
C. Wigglesworth.

Printed in the United States of America. All rights reserved. No part of
this book may be used or reproduced in any manner whatsoever without
written permission except in the case of brief quotations embodied in
critical articles and reviews. For information address Harper & Row,
Publishers, Inc., 10 East 53rd Street, New York, N.Y. 10022.

Library of Congress Cataloging in Publication Data

Wigglesworth, David C.   1927–   comp.
    Career education.

    1. Vocational education.   2. Vocational guidance.
I. Title.
LC1044.W53   375   74-25197
ISBN 0-06-453900-8

75   76   77   10   9   8   7   6   5   4   3   2   1

PREFACE

The honest critic of public education today is forced to admit that the general curriculum of today's educational establishments has failed to meet the needs of the majority of the enrolled students, the taxpaying society, or the needs of the community as a whole. The number of high school drop-outs and the large number of functional illiterates in our high school graduating classes attest, in part, to the failure of the general curriculum.

This book does not contend, nor does it intend to convey, that a Career Education curriculum will solve all of the ills (both real and imaginary) of the public schools. Nor does the text offer the Career Education curriculum as a panacea providing simplistic solutions to the myriad and complex problems within American Education. This *Guide To Career Education* hopes to light the reader's way to Career Education and to create sufficient interest in Career Education that the reader will be motivated to pursue the subject further.

Sidney P. Marland, former U.S. Commissioner of Education and later Assistant Secretary of Education has often been called "the father of Career Education." Yet, Dr. Marland has never promulgated the concept of Career Education as a panacea and in fact has been quite cautious in his remarks. However, many of the supporters of Career Education, both in and out of the U.S. Office of Education, have felt that they must present Career Education in a gilded framework in order to justify funds for its growth, development, and continuance. Unfortunately, this can create very real problems, for when any aspect of Career Education programs fails to meet the promised criteria of a panacea, it provides its opponents with the ammunition for its own defeat and destruction.

The contributors to this volume represent a wide range of backgrounds and interests. Their writings have appeared in diverse publications and their approaches to Career Education offer the reader a variety of exposures that may be instrumental in helping the reader to focus more precisely on the areas of Career Education that are of the most interest to him/her.

The book is divided into five sections: Introduction; Careers and the Schools; Career Clusters; Career Education Systems; and Career Education in Perspective.

In the introductory section there is an explanation of Career Education which provides some historical background, an explanation of the rationale of Career Education, and a description of the Career Education concept. This is followed by Dr. Marland's spirited championing of Career Education as "the most exciting trend in schooling today."

The introductory section also includes an exploration of the potential of Career Education, the relationship between Career Education and the School Curriculum, and a brief discussion of Career Education and the work ethic.

In the section entitled "Careers and The Schools," the reader is introduced to practicing examples of Career Education in action from kindergarten through junior college. Each of these articles provides an overview of the potential direction that Career Education might pursue. The different characteristics that emerge in each of these selections suggests one of the saving graces of our democracy that mitigates against authoritarian doctrines being promulgated from the nation's capital.

As Career Education programs develop in different communities around the nation they take on different characteristics which reflect the perceptions, thoughts, and needs of each particular local area. As a result, Career Education may not develop in exactly the same way everywhere, and the nation as a whole may benefit from the experiences of the parts. Thus the sum of the parts may be greater than the whole.

The Career Cluster concept is an integral part of the Career Education program and is one that will probably undergo constant revision. In this section of the text, the attempt is to present the clusters and define their areas, to discuss how they might be developed within an instructional framework, and to show how they relate to the world of work.

The Career Education Systems section approaches some of the concepts that are essential to the development of a total program that will be capable of relating effectively to students, teachers, parents, taxpayers, and employers.

Career Education in Perspective presents a dialogue between Dr. Marland and Dr. and Mrs. Caldwell that originally appeared in the *English Journal*. Upon reflection, it would appear that the Caldwells appear to be seeking many of the same goals as Dr. Marland but with somewhat different, though not necessarily diverse, emphases. To conclude this section Dr. Wanner introduces the European developments in Career Education that may have relevance and application to the programs within the United States.

The total book is designed to be a guide to Career Education that permits the reader to achieve an understanding of the various aspects of Career Education. It is hoped that the text meets this objective and that the reader will go on to more detailed studies of Career Education in order to reach the appropriate decisions for himself, his schools, his community, and his country.

The articles appear in their entirety except for certain instances where notes, bibliographies or figures have been omitted.

To the contributors to this volume and to their publishers who have so graciously granted permission for their reproduction in this text, go our sincere thanks for helping to guide us through an introduction to Career Education.

To Peter J. Verhoven and Dennis A. Vinton go special thanks for writing "Career Education" as the first chapter to *Career Education For Leisure Occupations*. It is by far the best short description of Career Education in its historical and educational perspectives.

Timothy F. Regan, now a Management Consultant with A.T. Kearney, Inc., provided access to specific areas of research, considerable research assistance, and warm personal encouragement which was much appreciated.

Sincere thanks are also due to Canfield Press for obvious reasons and to my Editor, Richard P. Thiel, for very deserved but less than obvious reasons.

David C. Wigglesworth
TRA Technical Research Associates, Inc.
Los Altos, California 94022

CONTENTS

PART 1

Introduction

A "briefing paper" published by the U.S. Office of Education defines the conceptual understanding of Career Education which ought to be kept in mind throughout this text. The paper states, "The fundamental concept of career education is that all educational experiences, curriculum, instruction, and counseling, should begin the preparation for economic independence and an appreciation of the dignity of work."

The concept of Career Education, generally ascribed to Sidney P. Marland, Jr., appears aimed at replacing the general curriculum of the public schools with a career or job oriented curriculum. It was Marland, who, in the November, 1971 issue of *American Education*, defined Career Education as "A concept that says three things: first, that career education will be a part of the curriculum for all students, not just for some; second, that it will continue throughout a youngster's stay in school from first grade through senior high and beyond, if he so elects; and third, that every youngster leaving school will possess the skills necessary to give him a start in making a livelihood for himself and his family, even if he leaves before completing high school."

In this introductory section, Peter J. Verhoven and Dennis A. Vinton present Career Education in historical, educational, and pedagogical perspective. Their article is followed by Marland's essay on "Career Education—The Most Exciting Trend in Schooling Today." John Letson explores the potential of Career Education and Dale Parnell relates Career Education to Maslow's theory of basic human needs. Parnell concludes that, "Career Education affords students opportunities to meet all the basic human needs—survival, security, belonging, self-esteem, and self-actualization. In this manner, the schooling experience will provide involvement and relevance because human needs will determine the purposes and priorities of education." The introductory section concludes with a short piece by Edie McConnell on the work ethic in regard to Career Education.

Peter J. Verhoven
and Dennis A. Vinton

CAREER EDUCATION*

Hank is in the second grade of a school where career education is included in the curriculum from kindergarten through high school. In keeping with the elementary school goals of career education, Hank is becoming aware of himself as an individual, his unique role in his family, and his family's role in the life of the community. Hank is learning respect for and interest in a variety of daily jobs performed by his parents, brothers and sisters, and friends of his family.

Judy, Hank's older sister, is in the eleventh grade of the same school. Career education there gives Judy an opportunity to select and study the work area in which she has the greatest interest and aptitude. Through professional guidance and counseling at school, Judy, who works well with people and enjoys leisure-time activities, has decided to pursue a career in the leisure field. The career education program in her school strives to prepare all students for placement, whether in a job, in post-secondary school job training, or in a four-year college.

No matter what Hank and Judy ultimately choose as careers, the subjects they study in school—English, mathematics, science, social studies, and the expressive arts—are designed to prepare them for their eventual working careers. They will visit job sites and observe the skills required on the job. They may be given the opportunity to work part-time at a job while attending school.

This brief scenario is what career education is all about. It is difficult to say when career education got its start, but the theories and concepts on which it is based are not new.

Educator Edwin L. Herr credits Benjamin Franklin with first recommending a combination of academic and vocational studies for youth of Philadelphia in 1759. The Industrial Revolution in the late nineteenth century intensified the emphasis on vocational training for America's growing middle class. During this period, and in the early part of the twentieth century, educator David Snedden advocated an educational system in which academic and vocational education would be independent but equal. He also encouraged the inclusion of specific programs related to the "actualities" of life and emphasized the economic advantages of vocational education.

*Peter J. Verhoven and Dennis A. Vinton—"Career Education" reprinted from *Career Education For Leisure Occupations, Curriculum Guidelines For Recreation, Hospitality, and Tourism* published in December, 1972 by the University of Kentucky under U.S.O.E. Grant No. OEG-0-71-4459 (357).

Charles A. Prosser and Charles R. Allen, pioneers in the movement to add vocational education to the public school curriculum, shared Snedden's interest in the economic aspects of vocational education. They believed it would provide skilled laborers for the nation's work force. At the same time, it would afford social and economic mobility to children of the poor through the teaching of practical skills to be used in securing and retaining jobs. Prosser and Allen supported the Smith-Hughes Act of 1917, which allocated federal funds to the states for vocational education.

However, critics of this theory charged that instead of promoting social and economic mobility, vocational training actually stifled it. They labeled vocational education undemocratic and a perpetuation of the status quo. It remained for John Dewey to offer an opinion of vocational education that has served as the basis for the development of the career education concept.

In brief, Dewey's theory held that if the child's knowledge began by doing, then vocational education provided the potential to satisfy his innate tendency to explore, to manipulate tools and materials, to construct and create. He believed that vocational education gave the child not only job skills, but also knowledge of the industrial world and the fundamental processes of economic life. In Dewey's view industrial education could be used as a correlating medium for other subjects, provided educators gave priority to educational values rather than industrial or vocational goals. He warned against taking vocational training out of the public schools. Separate trade schools would be dominated by industrial and commercial interests, he felt. Dewey believed that the educational values of vocational training, as presented by the public schools, would familiarize the student with the social and cultural background of his vocation as well as the skills involved.

During the depression years, the Civilian Conservation Corps (CCC) made a significant contribution to vocational education by giving job training to almost two-thirds of all CCC enrollees. The National Youth Administration of that era helped many a youth complete his education while earning a salary through part-time employment.

World War II, by involving most of the nation's young men in the military, forced the training of women, and others formerly considered unemployable, for productive jobs in all civilian work areas. During the war the military developed new screening and evaluation methods for placement of recruits. These psychological techniques soon found their way into civilian use.

Since World War II a major educational aim in this country has been to prepare the individual to become a contributing member of society. Some educators still feel that a general education will do the job. Others, however, accept current drop-out and unemployment figures as ample evidence that neither the teaching of pure academic subjects nor instruction in pure trade school skills is the way to achieve present-day educational goals.

The drop-out rate in high school has continued to rise since World War II. Unemployment figures remain at unacceptably high levels. With most schools offering traditional academic subjects as preparation for the world of work, many agree with educator Paul Goodman when he says that today's schools prepare the student for one thing—more school!

Only about three students in ten enter college upon high school graduation. What happens to the remaining seven? Only two of them receive any sort of career or vocational training. Former U.S. Commissioner of Education, Sidney P. Marland, summed up the situation in a 1972 speech to secondary-school principals in Houston, Texas:

> The vast majority of these youngsters (high school graduates) have never seen the inside of a vocational classroom. They are the unfortunate inmates, in most instances, of a curriculum that is neither fish nor fowl, neither truly vocational nor truly academic. We call it general education.* I suggest we get rid of it.

Many educators, including Commissioner Marland, believe that career education is a step in the right direction. Speaking before the Thirty-third Session of the International Conference on Education in Geneva, Switzerland, in September, 1971, Commissioner Marland described career education as follows:

> Career education is designed to give every youngster a genuine choice as well as the intellectual and occupational skills necessary to back it up . . . . Career education will begin as early as kindergarten . . . . As a youngster advances into junior high school, he will select three of fifteen occupation clusters . . . and begin exploring the nature of careers in each.
>
> By senior high school, he will concentrate on one cluster, developing sufficient skill in a specific occupation to qualify for a job . . . . Each student's program will retain sufficient flexibility to enable him to switch to a related occupation later with a minimum of additional training. In addition, each student in a career education program will always retain the option of going on to higher education.

The career clusters that comprise the world of work around which a career education program might be designed include:

Agri-Business and Natural Resources
Business and Office
Communications and Media
Construction
Consumer and Homemaking
Public Service
Fine Arts and Humanities
Environment

---

*It should be noted that Commissioner Marland was referring to the general tract and not to general education in its entirety.

Health
Leisure (Recreation, Hospitality, & Tourism)
Manufacturing
Marketing and Distribution
Marine Science
Transportation
Personal Services

Much of the support for the development and implementation of career education has been provided through the Vocational Education Act of 1963 and the 1968 amendments to that act.

Although there are several models being developed, the Comprehensive Career Education model, shown in the accompanying graphic display, has received the most widespread support and is the most fully developed. This is a school-based model sequenced in four levels, or phases: (1) career awareness; (2) career exploration; (3) career orientation; and (4) skill development.

A Comprehensive Career Education System

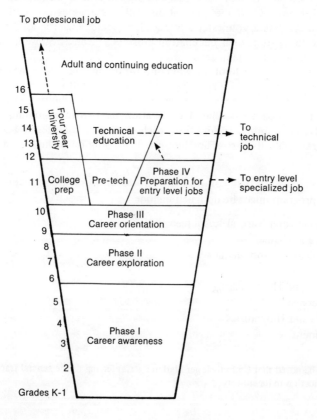

For each phase, a number of broad goals have been developed. Many of these goals are not bound by grade levels. For example, the awareness process implicit in Phase I continues through all grades. The major goals of each of the four phases follow.

Phase I (Career Awareness)

To develop student recognition of the personal and social significance of work.

To help each student become aware of himself as an individual and as a group member.

To develop student awareness of many occupations and to expand the career aspirations of each student.

To improve overall pupil performance by unifying and focusing basic subjects around a career-development theme.

Phase II (Career Exploration)

To provide experiences that will assist students in evaluating their interests, abilities, values, and needs as they relate to occupational roles.

To improve the performance of students by making basic subjects more meaningful and relevant through unifying and focusing them around a career development theme.

Phase III (Career Orientation)

To provide in-depth exploration and training in one occupational cluster, leaving open the option to move between clusters if desired.

To improve the performance of students by making basic subjects more meaningful and relevant through unifying and focusing them around a career development theme.

To provide guidance and counseling for students as they select eleventh and twelfth grade occupational specialties.

Phase IV (Skill Development)

To provide every student with specific, intellectual and practical skills in a selected occupational cluster or specific occupation in preparation for job entry and/or further education.

To increase the student's motivation to learn by relating his studies to the world of work.

To provide intensive guidance and counseling in preparation for employment and/or further education.

To provide placement of all students upon leaving school in either: (a) a job, (b) a post-secondary occupational education program, or (c) a four-year college program.

To maintain continuous follow-through of all drop-outs and graduates and to use the resulting information for program revisions.

Three Other Career Education Models in Various Stages of Development Are:

(1) the employer-based model; (2) the home/community-based model; and (3) the residential-based model. The U.S. Office of Education has described each of these models as follows:

The goals of the employer-based model are: (1) to provide an alternative educational program for students, aged 13-18, in an employer-based setting; (2) to unify the positive elements of academic, general and vocational curricula into a comprehensive career education program; (3) to increase the relevance of the world of education to the world of work; and (4) to broaden the base of community participation, particularly by involving public and private employers more directly and significantly in education. In fact, the program will be operated by a consortium of employers.

The home/community-based model will have three major components: (1) a career oriented educational television program with motivations to study for a career, and information concerning career opportunities; (2) home and community centered educational systems, using such media as cable television, audio cassettes, correspondence programs, radio and instructional aids; and (3) career clinics in the community to provide career guidance and counseling, referral services, and information on relevant career oriented education programs.

There is also a residential-based model. The Mountain Plains Regional Education Center, recently established at the Glasgow, Montana Air Force Base, will develop and begin to implement a residential career education program with services to disadvantaged individuals and their families. These families are being drawn from rural areas of six participating states which are seeking to develop their economies.

Family units are being brought to the training site so that each family member can develop an appropriate career role through employment, study, home management, or a combination of these methods. Employment upon completion of the residency is guaranteed by the home state of each family.

The material presented in this publication deals primarily with the implementation of a career education program for leisure occupations in the school. However, most of the guidelines are flexible enough to be used in planning employer-based, home/community-based, and residential-based career education programs, as well.

If all the Hanks and the Judys in our schools are to understand the world of work and to achieve what is their just right—preparation for their working careers—some changes must occur. The 1970 White House Conference on youth reflected this need for change in its report by stating that:

> The existing educational system, especially at the high school level, has failed to keep options for students to meet their individual needs, to adjust their educational curriculum as their interests and aspirations evolve and to adequately stimulate students in the pur-

suit of education. These failings have been especially acute in relation to preparing students to move into work . . . . Specifically the general education curriculum which typically prepares students for neither jobs nor college, should be phased out, and systems should be developed for integrating academic and vocational education curricula.

The career education concept offers promise that change will occur and the resulting program of education will provide many varied and broad avenues toward satisfying and productive careers for all of America's youth.

Sidney P. Marland, Jr.

CAREER EDUCATION— THE MOST EXCITING TREND IN SCHOOLING TODAY*

Career education—a concept that may still be new to many parents—has caught fire and is growing. Since parents should understand its many aspects, I welcome this opportunity to explain to them how it will affect their children and the schools, and how they can help.

Career education is not a gimmick; it is a total concept, a way of preparing youngsters for real life. But, though practical in its approach, career education should not be confused with vocational education. It is as important to the future of middle-class and well-to-do children as it is to the development of disadvantaged youngsters. It is a plan for everyone, whether in grade or graduate school and even beyond, to adult study.

To conform to the concepts of career education, elementary and secondary school curricula will be redesigned to lead youngsters slowly over the years into serious thinking about what sort of occupations they will be happy in later on.

Young people in the primary grades will be familiarized with basic information about occupations and will be helped to get exposure to work situations during the middle school years. Senior high students will develop marketable skills with which to enter their chosen field at graduation, or go on to college or technical training. Both post-secondary and graduate education will prepare individuals of all ages—as they do now—for broader career lives.

This early introduction to the world of work will offer an opportunity for youngsters to have real "hands-on" experience with various occupations of their choice before buckling down to one. Thus learning will become meaningful for them, directly related to their future as adults, and mathematics, English, history, and writing courses will be designed to meet their special goals.

The career education design eliminates the customary general high school curriculum altogether, and builds career orientation into the basic academic subjects all along the line, to help students choose from the 23,000 possible careers in

11

manufacturing, marketing, health sciences, communications, public service, the professions, and the trades. At the same time the student is receiving the necessary preparation for earning a living in a field of his selection at whatever moment he leaves the educational system. This moment might be graduate school or it might be before the end of high school.

As a parent, you can see at once what a difference this should make to the whole atmosphere of education. Some of you may have children well on in high school or even starting college, who have yet no idea of what kind of work—or even what kind of life—they want.

Conversely, your youngster may be the one who knows exactly what he likes and wants to do, but hasn't been helped in school to develop his interests and skills, much less apply them to dreams of a future.

It's true that the deficiences of our present system affect certain groups more harshly than others—ghetto youngsters, for instance, or migrant children—but children from educated, comfortable homes, children with above-average I.Q.'s, also stand to benefit from the new concept of career education. Coming from a privileged home does not of itself give a youngster the judgment or experience to light at once on a satisfactory career choice if his schooling has not helped him sharpen his tastes and abilities.

It is even possible that the business or professional man's son—or daughter—would really prefer to work with his hands rather than in his father's business or as a professional—if only some sort of stigma were not attached to that decision.

I know a young man who is in that situation. He is building models for architects and museums instead of being a banker like his father. The skills he is using to build models were acquired in an industrial arts course that captured his imagination in junior high.

What I hope for is a new direction in education to expose your child to a full range of career opportunities, to help him narrow down the choices, and then to provide him with the education and training he needs, fired by his own ambition and interests. Often that training would involve the "manipulative" skills commonly associated with vocational or technical education. It would be reinforced by curriculum in the traditional subjects which had been designed to serve a particular career field.

That hope of mine is a big one. To understand the size of the problem: each year nearly 2.5 million students leave the formal education system of the United States without adequate preparation for careers. In 1970-71 there were 850,000 elementary and secondary school dropouts, many of whom had found school pointless. In addition there were 750,000 general curriculum high school graduates who did not enter college and possessed no marketable skill. Of these who entered college in 1967, 850,000 did not complete the program in 1971, or finish any other organized occupational program.

The cost of this unproductive education, at $8,000 per child for schooling starting in kindergarten or first grade, comes to $28 billion or one-third of the entire $85 billion cost of education last year.

What cannot be estimated are the emotional costs to frustrated and floundering young people or the costs to the nation in losing their contributions. As a teacher and a person, I count the unfulfilled individual as a more serious problem than the high dollar cost.

A new Department of Labor study shows that during every year of the 1960's teen-aged unemployment was more than twelve per cent, with the rate for black and minority races running between 24 and 30 per cent. During the early 1960's unemployment among the sixteen-to-nineteen age group was three times greater than for adults 25 or over. By 1969, over five times as many teenagers were out of work as adults. If you are realistic, you will admit that your child might be part of these unhappy statistics, and that it is up to his school to give him a better chance to enter the labor force with confidence and self-knowledge.

All this is a tall order and more than any Commissioner of Education would attempt to deliver tomorrow. Career education cannot be a product of a single individual or federal office. It must be something that is understood and believed in by faculties, school administrators, boards of education, and especially by parents and students. Our role in the Office of Education is to support the concept and to help in its research design. For this reason, the Office of Education is developing four kinds of model career education programs to help schools, colleges, employers, and others visualize and begin to work out their own approaches and appropriate roles. In this we are being helped by people in business and industry, by labor leaders as well as educators and laymen.

The School-based Model

Career education was reorganized as a need in the six cities where the school-based model was funded in 1971-72. In special school districts in each of these cities—Mesa, Arizona; Los Angeles, California; Jefferson County, Colorado; Atlanta, Georgia; Pontiac, Michigan; and Hackensack, New Jersey—a cross section of pupils, staff, and parents was queried and the overwhelming reaction was positive.

The 15,000 questionnaires returned showed that in the six districts it is believed that career education can change a person's future, lower the high school dropout rate, and increase employment. There is faith in the staying power of the idea, and belief that elementary school is not too soon to think about a future occupation.

In the early grades in Mesa or Pontiac, teachers are trained to relate a science lesson to possible future careers in X-ray technology or oceanography. Course work in social studies may be related to courses in journalism, social work, the arts, politics.

As a child is counseled, and his strong and weak points and preferences considered, he gets a concrete view of clusters of kinds of jobs. The clusters may be related to a field trip to a newspaper, or explained as the many specializations involved in a visit to a shipyard, or any other area where the kinds of things people do every day show up in their great diversity.

Concrete experience is a necessity today, when fathers return home from jobs that often do not seem quite real. In the past, girls watched their mothers work at all the home skills they would need, and young men, in a simpler society, watched their fathers tend store, work with tools, or even practice law. Many young people formed their goals for the future around this study and observation.

In the junior high school career education plan, the six school districts encourage exploration of some of the more advanced career clusters. A student interested in public service or communications, for example, might be doing outside reading for his American government course. Field trips to state legislatures and television stations could be cued in. "Hands-on" experience through agreements with local business and industry might be planned for short periods or over summers to complement a youngster's school schedule.

By the time a student is ready to graduate in the six model school districts he will have made a tentative career selection and know where he is headed. If he plans to enter the health field, for example, he may have arranged for paramedic work as he trains at a technical school, or he may enter a college and look forward to pre-med courses.

In addition to these six model programs, there are about 100 mini-model career education projects now in operation, at least one in each state financed under the Vocational Education Amendments of 1968.

The Employer-based Model

This model forms a total educational program for youngsters from thirteen to eighteen who find current school offerings unchallenging and are often potential dropouts. It is an alternate system to the conventional schools.

Operated by a consortium of public and private employers, the employer-based program will use employer know-how and, where appropriate, facilities to provide both academic and job-related preparation. Students will either graduate from the program with credentials at least equal to those offered by the high school or return at any time to their home high school with full credit for work completed. Projects serving about 100 students each will get under way this fall in Portland, Oregon; Charleston, West Virginia; Philadelphia; the San Francisco Bay area; and perhaps one or two other sites.

The cooperation of business and industry is already impressive. In Charleston, West Virginia, for example, a city of under 100,000, ten employers have joined forces to operate a career education program for eleventh-graders. Among the firms are two banks, two brokerage firms, a hospital, and a department store.

The Home-based Model

This model is designed to reach out-of-school adults who want to train for new jobs. The approach will be to use TV and radio programs to encourage people to use the skill-training services already available in their own communities. Project staff will provide counseling, guidance, and some instructional services. The staff will also assess community effectiveness in providing career training and recommend new services as needed. So far, the Rand Corporation has analyzed four successful TV programs in terms of their compatibility for a career education series keyed to the home-based model. The Educational Development Center in Newton, Massachusetts, is studying the potential participants, developing an evaluation plan, and thinking through ways in which media and community efforts could mesh.

There are particularly strong possibilities in this model for new technologies. Special attention is being given to the use of TV cassettes for home use in self-teaching. Teen-aged mothers can study for their high school diplomas in this way. Housewives can train at home for careers or for re-entry into the market later on when their children are well established in school.

Residential Model

This form of career education is for disadvantaged families living in remote rural areas with few career opportunities. It provides the chance to move temporarily to a training center where every member of the family can learn new skills for employment, homemaking, or further study.

The first group of families is now being trained at a pilot center on part of an Air Force base near Glasgow, Montana. By this fall some 200 families should be in residence. The program is operated under a $4 million grant from the Office of Education to the Mountain Plains Education and Economic Development Program, Inc. The center serves residents of Idaho, Montana, Nebraska, North Dakota, South Dakota, and Wyoming.

Adaptations of the four models will be developed to suit particular needs. For instance, long ago New York State established its large regional high schools to serve the smaller towns and to bring together people from some distances. A school in Oklahoma is another example; young people come in by the week, are housed at the school, and develop their own career programs there. So, although we do not yet have a student-resident example in the group of models, I see great possibilities in this for small communities serving sparsely populated areas.

What will career education cost? It will be more expensive than our present system of schooling—twenty to twenty-five per cent above present per pupil costs for the first year. This money will be necessary to retrain teachers, develop teaching materials, add counselors, and expand services, including job counseling. We do not foresee many dropouts; students will leave when ready for work, or go into advanced education. After the first year or two the added costs of career education will sink to about five percent per pupil more.

There will be equipment costs because young people will have to be qualified in minimal ways before they can move out into actual concrete experiences. Equipment such as computers, printing presses, or medical equipment will be needed, and cooperation with employers will have to be sought for much of this, since most school districts could not afford such huge investments.

Businessmen and labor leaders with whom I have talked are sufficiently interested in the career education idea to indicate their willingness to help with the problems of equipment, as well as in other ways. They are deeply concerned with education and look to the schools for well-trained employees. It is possible that tax incentives might be given to businesses that cooperate in local career education. There might be new coalitions of school systems and industry in cooperative programs. In any case, financing is and will remain a state and local responsibility.

Labor leadership, too, seems to be cordial to the idea of career education. Key people in the labor movement are counseling my office regularly on the subject; they understand it and support its goals.

Labor leaders would surely raise some questions, such as, "Will high school students be brought into industry in competition with our workers?" We cannot do that, so we must plan some way around it, at the same time aiming toward offering real work experience to students. On the other hand, to use an example from one industry, nearly $60 billion goes into construction in this country yearly, and I understand that the figure could be increased by 50 per cent if there were able craftsmen to perform that work. The construction industry is earnestly seeking competent people.

Union membership or licensing should not be viewed as a door eternally closed to some. Union qualification can be part of the evolving relationship between the schools and industry, in which the schools take the responsibility of providing adequate training and labor collaborates in designing the curriculum. I would say, for example, that if a young black man, traditionally excluded from membership in many trade unions, becomes well trained in a field, the schools must help him find the place to use his skills. And I have every reason to believe they can.

What then can parents do to promote career education? Parents play an important role in influencing their growing children's attitudes toward a career. To begin with, parents should discourage the idea that "if you have a college degree you are somebody, and without it you are nobody." Merely attending college is not the answer, as we have seen from the college dropout records and lack of goals of many graduates. One mother from a well-educated family said she was grateful that, thanks to what she sees as a new trend, she feels less guilty than she once would have because her son wants to be an aircraft mechanic instead of a lawyer or doctor.

Basically, career education has the potential to provide lifetime training and education for people in an ever-changing technological world, where jobs rapidly become obsolete and new techniques must be acquired.

If you see career education as I do, as an important answer to many problems in schooling today, I hope you will become one of those activists to help us get it going.

Guiding young people to find the broad area of work they can enjoy their whole life long is no simple matter. It will require the patience to see them through a lot of early experiments. Your encouragement can help them; you can also see to it that productive people within the community have a chance to explain their occupations to a fifth, sixth, or seventh-grade class—a sort of adult "show and tell." You might even want to accompany your son or daughter to the various work-settings they now think they might like.

Beyond your immediate job as a parent, there is the community in which you live. If you are good at influencing people, start with your school principal, your district school superintendent, or the PTA and school board. Follow through to see that there are teachers and resources to implement a plan developing one of our models or creating one that is unique to your town or city.

I have described the models that the Office of Education has put into effect, but I particularly like the Dallas, Texas, model which has used no federal money at all. That city invested $20 million in the career education concept, starting its plan five years ago. During 1971-72, the first year of actual operation, over 40,000 students were involved. Their occupational clusters include the graphic, performing, and fine arts, construction, computer technology, and medicine. In the children and youth-related cluster, some students will spend up to three years in the kindergarten of Skyline Center, the Dallas complex which houses career education programs for young people and adults.

You can see that there is a lot for parents to do. They can also be participants, once career education gets under way. If a mother left school in her second year of college, say, to get married and start a family, now may be the time for her to return to college and aim for some satisfying work to do. Her educational plans can grow with the job.

By giving meaning and purpose to learning, career education is a way of continuing one's education throughout life. It is an idea that needs the help of all the parents it can get, all the parents who worry about what's in store for their children. If we agree to put career education into effect, we will have laid the groundwork for the many adaptations required of Americans in the 21st Century.

John W. Letson

THE POTENTIAL
OF CAREER EDUCATION*

Education has been both blessed and afflicted with innovative movements. New approaches have developed as the need for change has become apparent. In some instances the innovations gave promise of really revolutionizing the static patterns of the past. Some improvements did result from these various programs, but by and large education has undergone few fundamental changes over the years.

Many innovative proposals of great promise did not live up to their projected expectations because they were oversold as something entirely new and different. Career Education, however, is not really new or different. It is merely an effort to use a different kind of orientation for pupils in a belief that a new orientation can be the basis for stimulating a kind of response that the traditional academic approach has not achieved for approximately half of the student population. Also, Career Education is a concept that recognizes the urgent necessity of making sure that every pupil is prepared through education to find his proper place in the society and the economy.

For many, the increasing complexity of the world is baffling. Young people must make value judgments and career decisions on a much broader spectrum of possibilities and potentialities than ever before in history.

Although exceptions exist, the school usually assumes that its job is finished when a pupil drops out or graduates. It has not been generally recognized that education has a responsibility to make sure that all pupils make a successful transition to a job or further training or that the school has a responsibility to maintain a helpful relationship with them.

A report recently presented to the Atlanta Board of Education showed that all except about 200 of last year's graduating seniors either found jobs or were involved in additional training. In most cases, however, this was by accident rather than the result of anything we as a school system did to bring it about. Fortunately, the percentage of satisfactory employment was relatively high. But had we been able to include the employment rate among our dropouts, the

*John W. Letson—"The Potential of Career Education" from McClure, Larry and Buan, Carolyn, Editors, *Essays On Career Education*. Northwest Regional Educational Laboratory, April 1973. GPO stock number 1780-01147 (price $2.10). USOE/NIE Contract No. OEC-4--7-062871-3059. Reprinted with permission.

overall picture might not have been so favorable. To a small degree other public agencies are involved in helping pupils find jobs, but it is becoming increasingly apparent that the school must assume more responsibility for helping its pupils make the transition from school to work.

The time has come for education to answer some hard questions. The answers to those questions will determine the future of Career Education as a movement designed to bring about better and more relevant educational opportunities for all pupils.

To what extent is education oriented toward dignifying the whole spectrum of honest work? To what extent do we as educators leave the impression that success in life is inevitably related to college attendance? Is the high school curriculum broadly conceived to meet adequately the needs of all pupils—those who will attend college and those who will not—or is it heavily weighted in favor of the approximately 20 percent who will achieve a college degree? Is it possible to individualize instruction in a manner that adequately serves the needs of both groups, or must we continue merely to give lip service to this goal? Is an educational program that adequately serves the noncollege-bound groups inadequate for pupils who will attend a college or university? Has education lulled itself into believing that the traditional college preparatory program is the best way to stimulate and challenge able students to maximum achievement? Can we utilize a career interest to achieve a degree of pupil motivation and academic accomplishment not now a part of the experience of many pupils?

The answers to these and related questions constitute the purpose and goals of Career Education. However, we must not permit confusion about the term "Career Education" to develop, or this truly significant effort will be in danger of following the path of other promising but now forgotten innovations.

Career Education is not merely another name for vocational education. If it is so conceived, it is not likely to achieve its full potential. Students who will become research scientists, doctors, lawyers, engineers, or teachers are pursuing careers and are entitled to a preparatory program best suited to their needs. The discovery of better ways to assure maximum progress of all pupils toward their career goals is the purpose of Career Education. And the emphasis should be on "all pupils."

The traditional assumption that academically able students should go into the professions requiring a college degree and that those not academically talented should be guided into the vocational areas rapidly is losing its validity. It is becoming increasingly apparent, for example, that the same kind of ability is required to repair a computer as is required to develop and utilize a computer program. Despite this fact, our educational program and community values still assign a higher prestige to the man who operates a computer than to the man who repairs it. Hopefully, Career Education can contribute to the elimination of these artificial standards.

The popular assumption that vocational-technical programs were designed for the less able student is invalid, a fact that too many teachers and pupils still don't realize. Pupils, of course, frequently are influenced in this direction by their parents. Consciously or unconsciously, both parents and teachers often transmit the impression that jobs that call for manual skills are undesirable.

Are Atlanta teachers aware of the fact, and do they make it known to parents and pupils, that the city for the second straight year has topped the national list of housing permits per thousand population? Further, can teachers describe the thousands of jobs that support this industry?

By contrast, is it made known to pupils that Ph.D's also are numbered among the unemployed? Perhaps of greater significance is the educational program designed to make it possible for pupils to visit and talk with craftsmen and scientists about their work. Do teachers and pupils know, for example, that the average pharmacist spends 50 percent of his time counting pills, 10 percent of his time talking on the phone to physicians, and most of the rest of his time stocking shelves?

Possibly most important of all, do our students know the satisfaction to be derived from work well done? Can they, through experience, talk about the precision of a dove-tail joint or the poetry and beauty in a finished piece of furniture, and share with others the satisfaction of having achieved a perfectly adjusted engine?

It is unlikely that teacher or student has heard an orthodontist describe how a teen-ager beamed when the braces were finally removed, but such an experience is an important satisfaction to be derived from his profession. These essential parts of an educational program are not achieved through the usual academic approach. Career Education, on the other hand, seeks to incorporate varied, meaningful, and real learning experiences into the educational program of all pupils.

The fact that the traditional academic approach does not work for many pupils supports the urgent need for reorienting the educational process to eliminate this deficiency. Let me illustrate. I have asked on several occasions at schools whether or not pupils had been taken into the boiler room on a field trip. I have found that on many occasions pupils and classes went to the library to look at pictures of boilers, they read about steam and its generation, and they looked at films and filmstrips about steam and its properties. Seldom, however, have I found a teacher who led his class to the boiler room as a learning experience. Obviously, there is no magic about such a field trip. Nevertheless, the fact that such a field trip is seldom taken illustrates education's academic orientation as well as almost complete dependence on academic learning activities even when alternatives are readily available.

As I look back on my own school days, the things that I remember most vividly are the experiences that included an opportunity to see and feel and use materials or actually to participate in a meaningful activity. A pupil can read about chickens hatching in an incubator or under a hen, but if he has not actually seen it happen, it is less vivid and meaningful to him. To a large extent we have limited education to academic vicarious experiences. This academic process works well for only about half our students. We have mistakenly assumed that those who do not respond to the academic approach are unintelligent or that they can't learn. In most instances this is not true, but it is an indication that we have not yet discovered or implemented the educational process that will make it possible for all pupils to learn.

The present emphasis on Career Education is based on the belief that through the utilization of a career interest pupils can be motivated to higher academic achievement. At the same time, it is hoped that Career Education will accomplish the important purpose of helping students understand the opportunities that exist in the world of work. They should be able to do some realistic thinking about their own place in the world and how they can move step-by-step to accomplish their own goals. That is what Career Education is about. How effectively we move toward the achievement of these purposes will be related directly to the skill we demonstrate in translating the concept into action. I think it will be a serious mistake if we present, through a "Madison Avenue" approach, the impression that we are embarking on a dramatically new and different educational course. What we are talking about is what good teachers and good schools have been doing for generations. Simply, Career Education is the continued effort to discover those techniques, approaches, and curriculum content that will most challenge, stimulate, and interest all pupils.

The aim of Career Education is not necessarily to accomplish an early career choice. Neither is it envisioned that vocational counselors will give a series of tests and then confidentially advise pupils which career direction to take. This by itself is not good vocational counseling, and certainly it is not the goal of Career Education. Through a career emphasis pupils hopefully will have educational experiences that help them develop skill in making wise choices—choices that lead in the direction of personal responsibility, acceptable conduct, and appropriate performance in all areas of living. Career Education, if properly implemented, will provide an opportunity to redirect the curriculum to include a career emphasis as a means of stimulating and motivating pupils to higher achievement. Further, it will provide an opportunity to put into effect what we have long known—that first-hand, real experiences contribute to better learning than the typical academic experience of sitting passively at a desk attempting to absorb "an education."

As teachers, we should be able to devise creative activities that stimulate children and young people to progress academically and consecutively to develop an improved self-image through better understanding of career objectives and goals. Of course, it is easier to talk about such a goal than it is to accomplish it—the payoff is related to our ability to plan day-to-day activities that stimulate children and young people to maximum achievement.

It is most important that the Career Education concept be properly explained to parents. Recently, for example, a meeting of about 80 Atlanta parents was called to consider the organization of a private educational program because of misinformation about the Atlanta schools' emphasis on vocational education.

The parents in attendance assumed that *vocational* and *career* education referred to the same edcuational approach, that they did not want their sons and daughters taking vocational education. This, of course, reflected a misconception about the nature of both career and vocational education, but it clearly establishes the need for community involvement as the Career Education program develops. Regrettably, we have permitted vocational education to develop such an unfavorable image; it will be even more unfortunate, however, if we transmit this unfavorable image to Career Education through the use of the term as a synonym.

Through community involvement, parents must be assured that Career Education is not a program designed to channel young people into limited careers. Opening doors and keeping them open for all pupils would be a more accurate description of the career program. It is our general high school program that fails so miserably to open desirable career doors for so many.

I often have wondered what happened to the convictions of an earlier day that a brick layer who had the ability could become the largest contractor in the Nation. Has education helped to stifle the American concept that it is not where you start, but how you move from the point of beginning to where you want to go, that determines success and happiness, and that the option to take these upward steps is open to all?

Some will say, of course, that only the naive could hold such outmoded and old-fashioned concepts. They may be partially correct. But many illustrations prove that in part they also are wrong. Education is under an obligation to demonstrate that the opportunities exist. Hundreds of pupils-dropouts and graduates—are leaving our schools with little or no understanding of job opportunities. Many assume that the only place to look for a job is at a filling station or at a store. Too many are familiar with only those things they have seen.

Years ago when children walked down the street, they saw the blacksmith at work, the cabinet maker in his shop, and the agricultural pursuits of a calmer and quieter day being carried on by friends and neighbors. Today most work activities are carried on behind barriers pupils cannot see over. I have asked pupils, "What does your father do?" A typical answer is, "My father works at Lockheed." When pressed to explain exactly what his father does at Lockheed, rarely does a pupil answer with full understanding of his father's assignment. Certainly, this all too common lack of understanding of the world of work indicates an area of needed improvement. Education directed toward career interests offers a golden opportunity to make sure that all pupils are sufficiently well informed about the world of work to make wise personal choices.

As the Career Education concept is translated into day-by-day activities for pupils, it will become increasingly apparent that the school and the community it serves will join in a way that educators have long talked about. We still proceed in education as though it were better to sit in a classroom and read about something than to go and see it. One reason, of course, is that it is easy to do and is relatively inexpensive. Hopefully, the implementation of an educational program that utilizes career interest will contribute to moving the school into the community to a greater degree than is now the case. How this can be done best must be hammered out; but if a new relationship between the school and community results, it will be one of the valuable accomplishments of Career Education.

Again, however, Career Education must not be considered just another project to operate on the periphery of the school program. Changes do not come easily, but Career Education will not live up to its potential if it is conceived as something added on or as something supplemental to "business as usual." What is involved is the instructional process itself and how we can make it more meaningful for pupils.

The record speaks for itself as to the need for education to be made more meaningful for more pupils. Somehow or other, education too often has become the process of merely doing what the teacher assigns: do your homework, come to class and report, get more homework assigned to report on the next day. Individual motivation is too infrequently a part of the educational process, even though we know that it is easier to get pupils committed, involved, and concerned about those things *they* wish to accomplish. Career Education can become the instrument that stimulates a kind of educational program that is more self-directed—one in which every pupil can succeed.

It is really tragic that so many pupils leave school convinced they are failures. In this connection, Career Education offers no magic improvement. But if its potential is realized, it can result in better education for thousands of pupils.

Dale Parnell

CAREER EDUCATION AND THE SCHOOL CURRICULUM*

When bones become disjointed they are painful and demand attention. All of the rhetoric in the world will not bring the bones back into harmony or natural congruence with each other. It takes skillful, purposeful action, and you wouldn't be happy if the physician came within a bone or two of correcting the problem.

Likewise, when some major segment of society, such as schooling, becomes out of joint or in a state of disharmony with the needs of the individuals and the needs of society, it hurts and demands attention. We have many signals that indicate a lack of congruence between individual and societal "needs" and the results of schooling. Books, articles, television programs, and political speeches all are indicating to some degree, a sense of frustration with modern schools and colleges; indeed, they are expressing in various ways the need to build a greater degree of congruence into the education process.

Now, rhetoric may sell books and magazines, but it will not "rejoin the bones." That takes skillful action on the part of decisionmakers and managers in the educational enterprise. We must drive ourselves back to the beginning and take a good look at individual and societal needs and decide what we want schools and colleges to accomplish in relationship to these needs.

The simplest way to reorganize schools and colleges would be to leave the structure fairly intact but change the goals and reduce the slippage between needs, goals, and action. One fundamental principle that undergirds any organization has to do with goals. Everything in an organization must be measured against the goals and objectives of the organization. When goals and objectives are out of focus, actions of the organization staff and patrons tend to take on the same complexion. One of the reasons dissatisfaction often is expressed about modern schools is that we have failed to match in any systematic way the goals of schooling with the needs of contemporary individuals and modern society.

---

*Dale Parnell—"Career Education and the School Curriculum" from McClure, Larry and Carolyn Buan, Editors, *Essays on Career Education.* Ibidem.

Philosophical Base for Career Education

Maslow's Theory of Basic Human Needs

Abraham Maslow's theory of basic human needs provides an instructive insight for understanding the purpose of education. He contends that the human being is motivated by several basic needs. These needs are intrinsic. They cannot be killed by culture—only repressed.

Dr. Maslow postulates that the basic human needs are organized into a need hierarchy of relative potency. Throughout his life a person is always desiring something and "rarely reaches a state of complete satisfaction except for a short time. As one desire is satisfied another pops up to take its place."

Even though one cannot confine the need hierarchy to a literal and consistent posture, it can be stated safely that the basic needs generally are desired in a hierarchial order. Most individuals in American society have partially satisfied many basic needs, while still maintaining, unsatisfied, some basic needs that motivate and drive a person. Frank Goble has stated: "Dr. Maslow found that individuals who satisfy their basic needs are healthier, happier, and more effective, while those whose needs are frustrated develop psychopathological symptoms.

The most powerful and basic need is for survival—both physiological and emotional.

Dr. Maslow indicates that once the survival needs are satisfied to a degree, safety needs emerge. Any good teacher of young children has found that the child needs a secure world. When security and a degree of consistency are absent, the child becomes anxious.

With a predominance of survival and safety needs met, the needs for love and belongingness emerge.

The fourth level of need revolves around at least two aspects of esteem needs—self-esteem and respect from others. Self-esteem needs include competence, confidence, achievement, and independence.

Finally, Dr. Maslow finds that the need for self-actualization generally emerges after adequate satisfaction of the love and esteem needs. This highest level of need stems from that constant human drive to explore the human potential and nurture that potential into all it can become. In a later work, *Toward A Psychology of Being*, Dr. Maslow describes a whole list of higher-level needs he calls growth needs. However, it is important to point out that Dr. Maslow and many of his colleagues continue to state that this higher nature of man requires that the lower nature needs first be met.

Now, what does a hierarchy of needs have to do with the goals and purposes of schooling? The first purpose of the great American dream called universal schooling is to meet each individual at the point of his or her need. (Unfortunately, schools and colleges too often meet students at the point of *institutional* rather than *student* need.) One must look at the basic needs of human beings to gain an understanding of student need. If the first level of need is survival, does it make sense to force him or her to sit through the self-actualizing experiences of Shakespeare and Homer and ignore the survival needs? This is not to intimate that literature is unimportant, but only that if schools and colleges are to meet students at the point of their greatest need, the motivational aspects of the graduated scale of need must be recognized.

Human needs are motivational in nature and must be met, at least partially, in rank order. The postulate expressed here is that American schools and colleges often aim for the self-actualizing and higher-level needs while ignoring survival and security needs. What competencies are required to survive during the last quarter of this century? What kinds of competencies are required to cope successfully with life as a citizen, wage earner, consumer, and learner? Career Education can develop those competencies and help to meet basic human needs. This will mean that students will be different, that schools will be different, that teachers will teach differently, and that management will operate differently. If schooling can focus on the real-life career roles of individuals and the competencies needed to cope with those careers and roles, the immediate prospect is positive change.

Identification of Roles

A role is usually described as something that an individual performs throughout the course of his life. The role is defined by the expectations that an individual and others have for it as well as by certain ideal norms that society in general attaches to it. The roles of "life careers" with which all of us are simultaneously involved include the roles of being an individual (being myself, being an "I"), a family member, a producer, a consumer, and a citizen. (The role of being an individual would include such subroles as being a life-long learner; being a participant in avocational pursuits and leisure activities; and being aware of and committed to aesthetic, moral, health, and religious values.)

Relating Education to Roles

The question becomes, how does schooling relate to those roles? Successful performance in those roles requires more than knowledge; yet for some educators the main business of education is knowledge dissemination. Students could be told about their life careers or roles, and could memorize information relating to those roles. But that is not the same as the recognition that they are living those roles every day, in fact are experiencing those roles with or without the kind of schooling that would help enable them to achieve a measure of success and fulfillment—yes, even survival—in those roles.

Providing the kind of schooling that would meet that objective is the aim of Career Education.

The reason why Career Education as survival insurance is the most important educational trend today is clear enough: the educational establishment itself is finally convinced that traditional schooling is not meeting survival needs. An honest evaluation reveals that the modern schools are failing to meet a majority of the needs of a majority of students. The statistics are depressingly familiar and need not be cited here. However, one major reason for incomplete performance by schools is that many of our educational traditions stem from the first quarter of the 20th century and even earlier. Far too many of our educational requirements, including those for high school graduation and teacher certification, are based on the needs of the society of 40 or 50 years ago. Children, indeed, have outgrown present-day schools, as James S. Coleman pointed out in the title of his now-famous article in *Psychology Today*.

Dr. Coleman called the society of 50 years ago "information poor but experience rich." People received most of their information from books or from neighbors. But they were involved in all kinds of personal experiences through which they learned to know and to do the things that helped them cope with their kind of world. Children in the rural society were given chores, given responsibility; and, whether through trial and error or imitation, they learned practical skills and gained self-confidence and the respect of others.

Today we live in a different society—an information-rich society. In fact, children acquire so much information from television that many may suffer from *too much* data. They are not emotionally equipped to assimilate or interpret all they see and hear. They have not had the personal experience that provides realistic perspective. They see a president shot before their eyes and brutal scenes of wartime combat, but they may never have seen a dead rabbit or suffered the loss of a pet dog. When they enter the classroom they are confronted with even more information, often as ambiguous and generally less interesting than that on television.

How, then, can schools provide experiences that will enable students to relate information to living, to the real-life roles that constitute a part of living for all but a few of the most handicapped? That is the question that Career Education can answer. That is the essence of making schooling relevant to the total human need.

Career Education is wholly student oriented. It uses knowledge, values, and skills as a means to the students' ends, not as ends in themselves. In the Career Education curriculum, knowledge must be functionally related to the range of life careers or roles in which the individual will participate. In other words, it is education for survival in our contemporary society. That implies some rigorous demands and discipline, not just on and for students but on and for educators. It does not mean that everything will be easier. It does mean that student motivation based on a ranked order of needs will be a major consideration.

If Career Education is to work, a basic change in our attitudes must occur. We can no longer continue to give lip service to the American ideal of the dignity and worth of each individual and of our ability to provide equal educational opportunity for each individual to develop to his fullest capacity. We must believe it, and live it, and design school programs to fit it. Essentially, this must stem from the firm conviction that education is not knowledge alone. Education must include the right kinds of experiences, i.e., those experiences designed to meet the student at the point of his or her needs and enhance the potential for fulfillment in life roles. Concomitant to this, of course, is a commitment to the notion that schools exist to help students develop the competencies they need to negotiate real life at the survival level as well as the self-actualization level.

Career Education Is Not Vocational Education

Let it be emphasized again that Career Education is not synonymous with vocational education, although the latter is a significant aspect of Career Education.

American education has suffered from a misunderstanding of the place and value of vocational education. Unfortunately, the image in the minds of too many people is that vocational education is a group of boys gathered around an old car. Instead, it is a way to help young people develop the competencies they need to be wage earners and producers. It must be one of the primary goals of schooling.

New Competencies Demanded

If one can accept the premise that schooling must help students develop the competencies to cope successfully with life roles, then it follows that life roles must be examined. What competencies are required? Have life roles changed much in recent years?

Compared with 50 years ago, there are fewer, larger, and more complex units of government for today's citizen to understand.

Today's young citizen is faced with high-speed automobiles, freeways, and an abundance of alcohol and drugs. He must be concerned with physical survival in a very real sense.

The rural-urban shift has brought a proliferation of zoning laws. How many people understand them?

Students are voting at age 18. They know about George Washington and the Incas of Peru, but do they know how their city council or school board works?

Fifty years ago, when school requirements were established, no one carried credit cards. Are young people being prepared to cope with today's installment buying, contracts, insurance, and advertising tactics?

Do they know how to protect their rights as consumers?

One frequently overlooked role is that of the individual as learner. How much learning should come from the traditional classroom situation and how much should come from television or real-life experiences, such as work and travel?

A high school diploma is a minimal prerequisite for getting a job in many areas of the business world. But to be meaningful in this society, the high school diploma should specify what competencies the student has demonstrated. For the student who will want to work in manual or craftsman-type jobs, let's stop requiring more years of schooling and concentrate rather on strengthening the 12 years he now receives.

Ivar Berg, in his book *Education and Jobs: The Great Training Robbery*, challenges the notion that "education pays, stay in school." This notion has permeated society in negative as well as positive ways. It has caused unnecessary upgrading of educational requirements for jobs and an increasing surplus of educated people in relation to the jobs available.

In his study, Berg found that years of formal schooling are not significantly correlated to job performance; training on the job is more beneficial in terms of performance than credentials; and teachers with more degrees or schooling are not necessarily better teachers. He concluded that we ought to do a better job of educating all people with 12 years of schooling instead of spending large amounts of money in higher education for a select few.

Traditionally, we have furthered the undesirable and counter-productive separation of the vocational education, general education, and academic curriculums in our high schools. The result of this separation is that those in the vocational curriculum often are seen as low-status technicians, while students in the academic curriculum emerge with little contact with, preparation toward, or qualification for the world of work.

Changing Our Priorities

What changes can be anticipated in the schools as a result of clear goals and emphasis on helping students develop the competencies to fulfill successfully all life roles, particularly the role of wage earner?

Today we are dealing with a minority of needs of a minority of students. We must start again at the beginning and reexamine what schooling is to accomplish. Basically, we are still a cottage industry in education. About all that holds this "nonsystem" together are a lot of able teachers and hard-working administrators.

What can we do to meet a majority of the needs of a majority of students? The answers to this question are suprisingly pragmatic.

Decisionmaking Should Occur in State Legislatures

Clear signals are required to remove the fuzziness about the results desired from schooling. Each state legislature must review the general goals and purposes of schools and colleges. Until recently educators have gone to the legislature and said, "Give us money. Don't tell us what to do, just give us more money." What would you think if you went to a store to buy something and the clerk said, "You just give me the money and I'll give you what's good for you"?

Legislators don't want to have to involve themselves with specifics, but they do want some choice in deciding what they are buying. It seems perfectly legitimate for legislators to tell educators *what* to accomplish, yet with a further charge, "You figure out how to do it." This is the type of access to decision-making legislators can and should have.

Here is the kind of goal a legislature might consider writing into law:

> The education of the elementary and secondary school student results from a combined effort of home, church, and community. It shall be the *primary* responsibility of the schools of this state to help students develop individual competencies to function as *citizens, consumers, producers,* and *lifelong learners.* The schools have shared responsibility and a *secondary* role in helping students with physical, social, emotional, cultural, and ethical-moral development. It is important the schools support and reinforce the home and other community institutions in these areas.

With these priorities in mind, educators can begin to update school requirements and to define areas for which schools should be held primarily accountable. Under the present system the public holds schools accountable for results they haven't the remotest possibility of producing. Schooling must look at survival needs like helping the student become a wage earner or a wise consumer first and other needs second.

Guidelines Can Be Developed by State Departments of Education

Once legislative goals are established, State-level educators must exercise leadership by planning how these goals can be reached.

To implement Oregon's first priority goal to improve Career Education, local districts were asked to spell out in their own local plans where they were, where they hoped to be in 5 years, and what processes they would use to get there. They were asked to identify feedback indicators to be used to measure progress. Districts were encouraged to use the State plan as a suggested blueprint for designing their own plans as they wished. Once their plans were filed with the State board of education, they became the minimum legal standards for achievement in each area.

In an effort to make schooling more relevant to the needs of the 1970's, Oregon's high school graduation requirements have been subjected to the most thorough revision in 50 years. Under the proposed new requirements, exposure to a subject for a required length of time is not enough. Instead, the student must demonstrate competencies as a consumer, a producer, a learner, and a citizen. If the student leaves school early, he or she will be issued a certificate showing what competencies he has demonstrated by the date of his departure.

To encourage a student to prepare for an occupational role, he or she is being required to earn one high school credit in a cluster or family of occupations. Expanded vocational education programs have won widespread acceptance. In 2 years, Oregon has doubled enrollment in high school vocational education or career cluster programs and in community college courses as well.

Citizenship education is being separated from social studies. Students are encouraged to work for school credit in community service. Many students are learning about their communities by working with city councils, school boards, elementary schools, nursing homes, hospitals, and other components of the community. This experience will help them develop competencies for citizenship and a feeling of responsibility and pride in their communities.

The System Is Designed to Motivate Students

Today, formal education seems to be the passport to full citizenship; school credits, diplomas, and licenses seem to be the milestones. Schooling literally has become both a bridge and a barrier between an individual and his ability to earn his living. Without adequate schooling, a citizen is economically obsolete before he begins to work. But much traditional schooling is unrelated to the real world. Small wonder our present approach to universal education sees many young people bored, restless, and provided with few opportunities to relate school life to real life and the hierarchy of human needs.

William Glasser has observed that the most common characteristic of delinquent young people is hopelessness and goalessness. They may be intelligent and physically attractive, but because they rarely experience success they cannot imagine that they will succeed in the future. It has been the experience of this writer that the vital ingredients for a successful schooling experience are involvement and relevance. Glasser has found in questioning thousands of students that they did not see much value in most of the material they were expected to learn. When pertinence and meaning are present in the curriculum and daily school experiences, students will be motivated to learn.

While recently helping my son register for his first year in high school, a revealing syndrome came to light. This particular high school required the student to indicate on the registration form the selection of a track. The first track was "advanced or college prep," the second was "terminal," and the third was "remedial." Our response was easy. We sent the registration form back to the school and asked for more choices. We wanted real-life options, not a sorting system that gives the college-prep program top billing.

Walter Lippmann has said that we all operate on the basis of pictures in our heads, not on real facts. Unfortunately, we've developed in the schools and in the minds of the public, some images that demand correction.

For example, one image dictates that the important thing in life is to teach in the university; if you can't do that, you teach in a high school; if you can't do anything else, you teach in an elementary school. In fact, in terms of raw human need, the most important teaching job in all education is in the primary grades. Nothing in education is more important.

How about the high school tracking system? Regardless of our rhetoric, we indicate that preparation for college is advanced and everything else is second best. This system must be replaced by emphasis on life roles with Career Education providing the relevance, the involvement, and the motivation.

Teachers and the Curriculum Will Change

First, all of basic education must be infused with practical examples from the world of work and life roles. Even students in the primary grades must be able to see some relationship between what they are learning and the utility of that learning. Indeed, career awareness in the elementary schools should bring more life, more meaning, more experience, and more rigor to these early schooling experiences. Why not develop readers and library collections around world of work themes?

The real challenge to the American elementary and secondary school teacher is to infuse his or her daily teaching with practical examples from labor, business, industry, military, government, and home. The real challenge is to indicate to students how what they are studying measures up to life and human needs.

Of course changes in teacher education will be necessary if Career Education is to function in the classroom.

Second, career exploration in the middle grades can bring new purpose to those difficult adolescent years. Exploration does not mean that students will visit a little in the community or that they will talk a bit about jobs. Career exploration demands a multi-disciplinary approach with industrial arts and homemaking teachers leading the way. The new industrial arts program will explore all of the clusters and families of occupations, of which some 15 to 18 with such titles as health occupations and mechanics occupations are identified. Boys and girls in the middle years should be able to explore all of the clusters, not just some of them. Generally, the industrial arts program has been limited to boys dealing with metals, plastics, electricity, and wood.

The challenge for the industrial arts program is to bring girls into the program and provide more meaning and more vigor for the total middle-school curriculum. For example, in the world of construction the building of a bridge can be a beautiful example. Teachers must not only *talk* about the occupations involved in mixing mortar and cement, they must let students lay up a brick wall and experience the mixing of mortar. But that isn't all. The illustration of building a bridge provides tremendous opportunities for basic education disciplines. Who planned the bridge and how was the planning done? How was money raised to pay for the bridge? These and similar questions can stimulate exploration of a great many important questions related to the basic survival skills mentioned earlier.

At the end of a 3- or 4-year period, students will have explored all the major clusters or families of occupations and had actual working experiences related to significant aspects of these occupations. They also will have begun to understand the relationships involved between economics, mathematics, communications, and other disciplines.

The third major change needed is to integrate what has been called general education with Career Education in the secondary schools by following the career-cluster approach. The career-cluster concept is aimed at the development of skills and understandings that relate to a family of occupational fields. To put it another way, a cluster of occupations is a logical group of selected occupations, related because they include similar teachable skill and knowledge requirements. High school education, then, will be centered primarily on the knowledge and skills common to the occupations that comprise a cluster or family. This not only serves as a motivational tool but will prepare students for entry into a family of occupations rather than into a specific occupation.

One of the most critical needs in Career Education today is for the high schools, community colleges, and technical-vocational schools to articulate and coordinate preparatory and specific career training programs. Secondary schools should offer preparatory Career Education and training. Community colleges, private vocational schools, apprenticeships, and on-the-job training programs should offer specific job training and should coordinate the other nonschool on-the-job training program efforts. Secondary schools must concentrate on career training in the broad-cluster concept rather than specific job training. Students should be able to select a career cluster at the beginning of their high school experience and then tie a majority of their high school experiences into this generalized goal. This will not involve so much a change in facilities or curriculum as a change in guidance and counseling patterns and a change in the way a secondary school curriculum is outlined.

What we are really calling for is a change in thinking so that preparation for a career becomes accepted as one of the clear and primary management objectives of the secondary school.

In the future, a student's Curriculum "menu" is likely to include the following career-cluster options: accounting, agriculture, clerical, construction, domestic and custodial, electrical, food service, graphic arts, health, marketing, managerial mechanical and repair, metals, secretarial, social services, textiles, transportation, and wood products.

A well-planned and successful Career Education program also should have great impact on teacher morale and on professional pride and satisfaction. In all the criticism of public education, much is made of incompetent instruction, apathetic educators, resistance to innovation, and other negative observations. Seldom do we stop to think that teachers are a dedicated group. Many entered education because they were idealistic and wanted to help young people. The majority of teachers sincerely want their students to develop to their fullest potential. But teachers have been frustrated—as frustrated as their students—because the educational system itself has unwittingly foiled some of the best plans to improve education. So, if in a Career Education program teachers begin to see young people grow and blossom the way we all want them to, there is built-in satisfaction guaranteed for all concerned.

Nontraditional Facilities Will Be Utilized

Comprehensive Career Education calls for new concepts of the use of space and time. This does not mean widescale tearing down of our present school buildings and replacing them with wholly redesigned facilities. It does mean rethinking our use of present facilities, however. For example, does a food-service career-cluster program require construction of new kitchen facilities, or can the present school cafeteria be utilized as a laboratory?

Since Career Education includes much more than vocational education, some of the learning in a Career Education program takes place outside the school building and in the community. Citizenship education, consumer education, and education as a family member can include much work in the living labora-tory—the real world of shopping, voting, and contributing services to others.

So part of the impact on schools will be a much greater use of space (all the community space around the school) and much more free and flexible use of time. For example, a student might work on a hospital night shift for class credit and not be expected at school until 1 p.m. the next day.

Furthermore, as schooling moves out into the community, the community will move into the schools. This means that community members with expertise in various areas will be brought in to join the teaching team and share in the learning process of students. The year-round school idea will gain wide accep-tance as a result.

It is entirely conceivable that the 12th grade will be spent in a nearby com-munity college, in on-the-job training, or in community service. The secondary schools and the community colleges must analyze their facilities and determine areas of cooperation.

High school work done at community colleges might fall into two categories: (a) the advanced-placement type where high school students can attend a nearby community college and take an occupational program and receive college credit for it; or (b) shared time, shared instructors, and often, shared facilities.

Federal Educational Agencies Should Play a Role

Sidney P. Marland, Jr. has given the notion of Career Education a gigantic push forward by his support. But at least five additional steps must be taken to assure that progress is balanced and swift. It is imperative that each State not be required to reinvent the wheel. Tasks to which the National Institute of Education and the U.S. Office of Education might address themselves include:

1. Identify priority human needs and build a solid, clearly stated philosophical base for Career Education around these needs.
2. Identify points of intervention in the schooling process that promise high level payoff. Where can local school boards achieve the greatest return for their investment? Intervention points that need research and consideration include registration forms and school placement procedures, library books and materials, principals, textbooks, parent handbooks, curriculum guides and catalogs, local and state board policies, and high school graduation requirements.
3. Identify and validate what is really working in American education as related to the initial goals of Career Education. Such a search must include looking

at work going on in community colleges, proprietary schools, the armed services, manpower development and training, and multi-disciplinary materials. Not only must the search look at materials, but at exemplary classroom practices. A catalog of exemplary practices and related objectives would be most helpful.

4. Develop some simplified feedback indicators that can be used as evaluation tools for examining the results of Career Education efforts and as instruments by State and local school districts.

5. Continue to examine the excess costs of Career Education, particularly in developmental stages, and present such information to Congress. As a minimum, Congress should be requested to maintain the per-student level of funding that existed prior to the present emphasis.

Conclusion

By giving young people opportunities for various real-life experiences, we also will approach indirectly several problems. Traditionally, we have tried to attack emotional, racial, ethical-moral, and cultural problems directly, by telling people what to do—telling them to be moral, for example. Instead, schooling must do more than telling. It must provide opportunities for students to experience and cope with real situations.

Hopefully, today's student can begin to feel more confident about himself by developing competencies. He can feel tolerant toward others by developing the skills needed for coping with life. We will provide him a healthy atmosphere as rich in experiences as in information. Thus, schooling of the 1970's and 1980's will indeed equip students with survival competencies to enable them to act as independent, contributing citizens in the remaining decades of the 20th century.

Career Education affords students opportunities to meet all the basic human needs—survival, security, belonging, self-esteem, and self-actualization. In this manner, the schooling experience will provide involvement and relevance because human needs will determine the purposes and priorities of education.

Edie McConnell

CAREER EDUCATION AND THE WORK ETHIC*

"If anyone will not work, let him not eat."

St. Paul

"A man is a worker, if he is not that, he is nothing."

Joseph Conrad

"In idleness there is perpetual despair."

Thomas Carlyle

"God intends no man to live in this world without working; but it seems to me too less evident that he intends everyman to be happy in his work."

John Ruskin

"All paid employment absorb and degrade the mind."

Aristotle

"I like work; it fascinates me. I can sit and look at it for hours."

Jerome K. Jerome

The word work means many things to many people. Americans, through a philosophy passed down from St. Paul to the Reformation and the Puritans, have embraced a work ethic—work for the sake of working is good—that seems to have been challenged recently.

At the convention of the New York State Home Economics Association last year, author and educator Neil Postman predicted that, through technology, by the year 2000 there will be jobs that contribute to the economy for only 50 per cent of the population. The work ethic that man must work to eat, he said, is one of the beliefs that Americans are going to have to "forget" in order to survive.

Whether or not Mr. Postman's prediction is correct, the idea of work for work's sake is being challenged. Early retirement is the goal of many. A recent

*Edie McConnell—"Career Education and the Work Ethic" reprinted by permission from FORECAST For Home Economics, copyright ©1973 by Scholastic Magazines, Inc.

Time article gave some revealing statistics about work in the U.S. Since the early 1960s, absenteeism at auto plants has doubled to 5 per cent on Mondays and Fridays. Unions report that more and more members value leisure and are refusing overtime work at time and a half. People, even the unemployed, are becoming more particular about the kinds of jobs they have. Even with un-employment over 5 per cent there are shortages of domestic workers, taxi drivers, plumbers, and auto mechanics in some areas.

On the other hand, it remains that 90 per cent of all men in the U.S. between the ages of 20 and 54 work or are actively seeking work. The figure of married women working has risen in the past 20 years from 25 to 45 per cent.

A Yankelovich survey of college students revealed that 79 per cent believe that commitment to a career is essential. Only 30 per cent said they would like to see less emphasis on hard work in the U.S. and 75 per cent believe that it is immoral for a person who is able to work to collect welfare.

It seems then, that perhaps it is not work itself, but the quality of work that is being challenged. A recent Gallup poll revealed that 19 per cent of all American workers are not happy with their jobs. In 1969 the figure was 13 per cent.

A study done by the University of Michigan Survey Research Center asked a group of working people to rank different facets of their work in order of importance. They listed: 1) interesting work, 2) enough help and equipment, 3) enough information to do the job, 4) enough authority to do the job, and 5) good pay. Evidently the actual job satisfaction was more important to them than the monetary reward.

The monotony and boredom of many white and blue collar jobs is growing. A recent study by the Department of Health, Education and Welfare reports that a few companies in the U.S.—General Foods, Corning Glass, General Electric, Polaroid, American Telephone and Telegraph, and Texas Instruments—are engaging in experiments with a small number of their employees that seem to alleviate these problems and give greater job satisfaction.

At the General Foods pet food plant in Topeka, Kansas, factory workers are getting the opportunity to decide how to spend their time.

The workers in the plant have been divided into teams of about 10, each with a leader. The team leaders have authority similar to a supervisor except that they meet with other members of the team to make their decisions. The members of the teams work at different jobs at different times, so they learn all the jobs from unloading grains to working a control panel. Each team decides who will work each job, hires new workers, and makes most of the decisions affecting their area. The workers like the responsibility.

Other companies are giving employees more responsibility.

Indiana Bell, for example, used to divide 17 separate operations among a staff of women when compiling its telephone books. Now each worker is in charge of her own directory and performs all 17 tasks. The company says that turnover, errors, absenteeism, and overtime have all declined.

The H.E.W. report on work emphasized that jobs need to be enhanced, not only out of the self-interest of corporations, but also to improve society. It said that business should be held responsible for such social costs as political aliena-tion, aggression, alcoholism and drug abuse, mental depression and physical illness, which some researchers have tied to dissatisfaction with work.

Although a few companies are experimenting and some have made basic reforms that give workers more responsibilities, opportunities to learn, and a voice in determining what and how they will do their work, the movement is not widespread.

Giving workers more than one task to perform, letting them organize their own work and set their own hours, breaking up the assembly line and letting them see the end product of their work are the basic factors that experimenters think will not only alleviate job dissatisfaction but produce better products and profits.

Another means of changing the structure of work and increasing job satis-faction is through education. This education is especially important in erasing the attitude pervading our society that non-college degree jobs are second-class jobs.

Educator William Loomis wrote in *American Education*: "The condescending attitude toward vocational education has been a principal factor in creating the present imbalance among vocational, general, academic courses in high schools throughout the country. Last year, some 70 per cent of all 11th and 12th grade students were enrolled in general and academic courses; about 30 per cent were enrolled in vocational education courses. Yet we know that only 20 per cent of American youth can reasonably expect to finish four years of college and receive a bachelor's degree; still, society continues to dictate that a college degree is essential to job security and status. Parents continue to want their children to go to college and achieve 'success' in society's eyes."

Perhaps it is this "success ethic" that is being challenged by the young more than the work ethic.

Vocational education as we know it has not really lived up to its potential. High school students need to be given the opportunity to look into as many occupations as they want before choosing the one they will pursue. In some vocational curriculums they get "locked" into a subject that they find they do not like or does not suit their abilities.

Sidney P. Marland, writing in *School Shop*, stated, "We must provide far more flexible options for the high school graduate to continue on to higher education or enter the world of work, rather than sustain the anachronism that he must have made his career choice at age 14."

Schools in the U.S. have divided their curriculums into "college preparatory" or "academic" and "vocational" categories.

This division, says Loomis, has placed vocational education in a second-class position. "All too often, vocational education has been a euphemism for 'loser' and academic education a label for 'winner,'" he stated. "This . . . division must be eliminated if education is to achieve one of its principal aims and prepare our young people for meaningful employment."

It has been estimated that by 1975 more than 17 million Americans will be enrolled in vocational education at secondary, post secondary, and adult levels. In order to maintain the present teacher ratio—which isn't very good—of 50 to 1, the number of teachers will have to be increased from 172,000 to nearly 350,000.

Teachers are needed with the background and skills to prepare students for job opportunities—not only existing jobs but future ones.

Students need guidance in discovering their abilities and goals and then in pursuing the various options available to them. Home economics—through preparing students for the world of work both in "general" and "occupational" courses—has much to contribute to a vital ingredient of job satisfaction—career education.

PART 2

Careers and the Schools

The United States Office of Education has established Career Education as a national priority. According to the U.S.O.E., the salient features of Career Education include: the restructuring of basic subjects around the theme of career development; extensive guidance and counseling for decision making in career development; and studying careers in relation to major fields of occupations so that students leaving high school will be better prepared for either employment in a job of their choosing or additional education in institutions of advanced standing.

The career goals of the K through six program of instruction are: to develop the students' self-awareness and career-awareness; to expand their occupational aspirations; to develop decision making skills; and to develop appropriate attitudes about the personal and social significance of work.

The middle school or junior high school program of instruction should further build upon these goals. Therefore, the middle school, or junior high school program should include opportunities for students to evaluate their interests, values, and abilities as they relate to occupational opportunities and career lines. The process of evaluation of selected occupational clusters or groups is achieved through basic exploration and orientation in the middle school which become the foundation for in-depth exploration and beginning specialization of a particular cluster or group. From this base of knowledge and experience, students can begin to specialize in a cluster, family or group of occupations.

According to U.S.O.E., a kindergarten through post secondary developmental program in Career Education seeks to accomplish the following objectives:

To develop in pupils attitudes about the personal and social significance of work.

To develop each pupil's self-awareness.

To develop and expand the occupational awareness and aspirations of the pupils.

To improve overall pupil performance by unifying and focusing basic subjects around a career development theme.

To provide experiences for students that will assist them in evaluating their interests, abilities, values, and needs as they relate to occupational roles and career lines.

To provide students with opportunities for further and more detailed exploration of selected occupational clusters, leading to the tentative selection of a particular cluster for in-depth exploration at a grade level functionally equivalent to the ninth grade.

To provide in-depth exploration and training in one occupational area, providing a foundation for further progress, yet leaving open the option to move between clusters, if desired.

To provide guidance and counseling for the purposes of assisting students in selecting an occupational speciality for grade levels functionally equivalent to eleventh and twelfth with the following options: intensive job preparation, preparation for post-secondary occupational programs, or preparation for a four-year college.

To provide every student with intensive preparation in a selected occupational cluster, or in a specific occupation, in preparation for job entry and/or further education.

To provide intensive guidance and counseling in preparation for employment and/or further education.

To insure placement of all students, upon leaving school, in a job, a post-secondary occupational education program, or a four-year college program.

To maintain continuous follow-through of all dropouts and graduates and to use the resulting information for program revisions.

In essence, we are exploring the possible, or even probable, revision of the general *curriculum* in terms of Career Education. It is important to stress at this point that we are talking of the general *curriculum* which should not be confused with general *education*. Any serious revision of the general curriculum in the area of Career Education suggests that the schools will be deeply involved in evaluating the world of work in order to identify and pursue the development of the component parts of a program that will meet the needs and goals of Career Education, as outlined above.

The articles in this section of the text are concerned with the schools and career programs and relate concepts and experiences that are developing within specific school districts in different parts of the nation.

Dorothy Madlee, a Florida journalist, reports on the Orange County program in Florida and relates a number of significant changes that have occurred within the schools and the community. She relates the effect of the program on the schools, teachers, parents, students, employers, and the community as a whole. It would appear that Career Education in this particular project has functioned as an agent of change with far-reaching effects within the community.

Dennis T. Torp, Administrative Assistant, Warren Consolidated School District, Warren, Michigan, discusses the Career Education thrust and relates the experiences of the Warren Schools in the utilization of a three phase approach that incorporated activities and concepts already in operation. This helped to provide an overall pre-planned program prior to implementation.

Robin Pierce, a former high school English teacher and now a free-lance journalist, writes about the implementation of computer technology in a secondary school level Career Education program. The Eugene, Oregon OIAS (Occupational Information Access System) is an information and counseling program that plays a significant role in Career Education program development.

The Dallas High School Skyline program has been described in many publications and journals and has received nation-wide attention. We chose to let the Superintendent of the Dallas High School District, Nolan Estes, report on the concept, implementation, and success of the Skyline program.

Marie Y. Martin, Director of Community College Education for the U.S. Office of Education, discusses Career Education programs at six community/junior colleges across the nation.

Following Dr. Martin's article is a discussion of the role of community colleges in Career Education. John F. Grede, Vice Chancellor for Career and Manpower Programs of the City College of Chicago, places the role of the community college in proper perspective and indicates that the community colleges may do well to assume a leadership role supportive of the Career Education concept.

Dorothy Madlee

CAREERS FROM
A TO ZOO*

For the past couple of years Florida's Orange County has been the destination of hundreds of thousands of visitors bent on tearing themselves out of the real world—if only temporarily—to explore the marvelous and assorted fantasies of Disney World. In odd contrast, Orange County is also the place where school children have an especially good opportunity to rid themselves of whatever fantasies they may have about the real world and to prepare for work in it. The point: There is no Mickey Mouse in the Orange County Career Development Program.

County educators are justly proud of their career program which is not only doing what they hoped it would do but has helped to restore the ego of one of the county's fine old schools, now called the Wymore Vocational and Technical Center. When Robert S. Megow was appointed principal of Wymore in 1967, he took over a school drooping from low student and teacher morale, falling enrollment, and a high dropout rate.

It had not always been so. The school in the all-black city of Eatonville, a few miles northwest of Orlando, had been known as Hungerford Academy, a black-owned private institution founded with the help of a gift from Booker T. Washington and maintained by endowments from blacks and whites. Its academic rating was high. It had given generations of black students their starts toward college and distinguished careers in medicine, law, education, and science.

The academy, then including nearby Hungerford Elementary School, survived the Depression, but in 1950 finances dwindled and the school was taken over by the Orange County school board, which renamed it and changed its curriculum from academic to vocational. The blow to Eatonville pride soon was reflected in school apathy.

Although the general population increased, enrollment at Wymore had shrunk from 800 to 250. Many students admitted they were merely waiting for dropout age—the 16th birthday that would free them from school.

"I knew something had to be done to revive the interest of teachers and students," recalls Megow, who is now director of the Orange County Career

*Dorothy Madlee—"Careers from A to Zoo" reprinted with permission from *American Education*, May, 1973. *American Education* is a publication of the U.S. Office of Education.

Development Program. Megow, a squarely built, ruddy faced man, wasn't quite sure what to do, but fortunately he was gifted with tireless energy and a determination to match. In the fall of 1970 with two of his teachers he visited the huge Beggs Educational Center in Pensacola, which he had heard was solving a problem similar to Wymore's by fusing academic and vocational subjects. This was in line with his own conviction that every student—white or black, well-heeled or poor—should be equipped to make a living. But this training, he felt, should be in connection with academic learning, not a choice excluding it.

Megow's next trip was to Tallahassee where he talked with Carl Proehl, head of the Vocational, Technical, and Adult Education Division of the Florida Department of Education. Proehl suggested that Megow write a proposal for Wymore, since U.S. Office of Education funds had become available for developing career-oriented programs and testing methods.

Drawing upon his staff and a group of enthusiastic elementary school teachers, Megow wrote and rewrote a plan that included kindergarten through 12th-grade. His reward: a $245,000 Federal-State grant, renewable for a total of three years.

The Orange County school board approved the plan in May 1971, and by July, 54 teachers who would be involved directly were getting the details at a workshop. There was to be one program teacher at each grade level in nine schools chosen for their pupil flow into Wymore: three junior high schools (Union Park, Winter Park, and Apopka) and their feeder elementary schools (Bonneville, Columbia, Hungerford, Killarney, Wheatley, and Lovell). The program would be headquartered at Wymore.

At first some principals and teachers were hard to convince, fearing the program might weaken their schools' academic standing. Many teachers hesitated to accept new treatment of their traditional subject matter. They feared also that parents—many already hostile over court-ordered desegragation—might be still more upset if the classic subjects were taught with an emphasis on how they apply to today's occupational world.

"People naturally resist change unless you can point to a record of results and say, 'Gentlemen, this is what we have done,' " Megow says. He credits success to those teachers who believed in the idea and wrote their own curriculums during the workshop. These believers went into the schools as development supervisors, promising reluctant teachers a flow of day-to-day lesson plans, materials, and arrangements for field trips and outside speakers.

Once the program achieved a foothold things became easier. "Many of the things we were doing spread to other classrooms because of pupil pressure," Megow says. "Teachers began to consider the program seriously after a number of pupils who had observed what our classes were doing would ask, 'Why can't we do interesting things like that other class does?' "

During the 1971-72 school year, enrollment at Wymore increased from 250 to 450 and the racial mixture balanced from 90 percent black to a 47 percent black—53 percent white ratio. The additional Caucasians were voluntary transfers from other schools, boys and girls from varied economic backgrounds who were more interested in doing than in abstract learning.

"We never discourage a student's plan for college," says John Horn, project consultant. "What we do combat is the old concept that the boy or girl who doesn't go to college is necessarily a failure."

Of 51 Wymore seniors graduated last year, 12 are now in colleges or universities, two are in technological schools, 30 are employed, three are seeking jobs. The whereabouts of the remaining four are not known.

Meanwhile the Orange County program has grown to where it needs 125 teachers; the county administration expects to install extensions in 19 additional schools this coming fall; and similar career program models have been introduced in Pinellas, Brevard, and Leon counties. Many other school systems, in Florida and elsewhere, are studying Megow's plan of flexible curriculums integrating academic subjects with the working ways of the adult world.

There are 15 occupational clusters, each taking in the varied jobs within a general field—mechanics, building trades, sewing trades, food service, child care, health occupations and horticulture are among them. One cluster is made up entirely of jobs within the humanities and arts "Historians, sculptors, musicians, and anthropologists work too," Megow smiles.

Each cluster begins with the simple "what people do" approach of the kindergarten and is carried through the early elementary level, through the increasing sophistication of junior high school learning experiences to the technical job training offered at Wymore.

"I feel strongly about this program," says James C. Peery, principal of Lovell Elementary School, where the 1,060 kindergarten through sixth-grade pupils are predominantly white and from lower middle economic backgrounds. "Before this started, you'd ask a youngster what his daddy did for a living, and the answer would be, 'He works.' Most of them didn't know, or if they could name the father's trade, they had no idea what it meant.

"It's part of our way of life, I suppose, to play down certain vocations—plumbers, electricians, clerks. We don't give these poeple much reason for pride. Fathers and mothers go off to work and come home tired and grumpy—in no mood to talk about anything interesting or challenging that may have happened that day. The children grow up with the impression that the grownup world must be pretty dreary. What's the hurry, they think, to learn and grow up just so you can join the snail race?"

Laurel Grundish, one of Megow's original nucleus of enthusiastic teachers, entered Lovell as career development specialist, fresh from the first summer workshop and its concentrated flurry of curriculum creation. She emphasizes the flexibility built into the format, allowing teachers and the specialist to take advantage of current situations and events of interest.

One class in the project had 28 boys, chosen because they were chronic absentees. To arouse their interest they were launched in a unit on jobs connected with the zoo. In this unit they took field trips to the zoo, were visited by an animal expert who talked to them of animal lore, and were encouraged to do their own research on wild animals. Zoo history was admixed with human history: the boys learned of the animals portrayed in drawings from old Egyptian tombs and in the animal collections of the early kings of Nineveh and of ancient Greeks and Romans; they studied zoos as civic institutions in medieval Florence.

Vocabularies and reading skills increased along with the boys' zest for discussing modern zoos and playing the roles of people they employ: grounds maintenance men, compound keepers, dieticians, veterinarians, operators of vehicles and concession stands, animal handlers, and caretakers. They took note of how zoos are planned for natural settings to afford comfort for animals and spectators, and how animals should be cared for and protected.

No matter what subject or skill the boys worked at, animals were the key: in art they drew animals in their native environment; in language arts they discussed animals they found particularly appealing and wrote stories about them; in arithmetic they computed such things as construction measurements for zoo compounds, expenses entailed in feeding animals, and concession profits.

Completing the zoo unit, the class switched to airports and the jobs they offer. But by this time absences had dropped sharply; over one period of 15 days the boys established a record of perfect attendance. Throughout the year, only real illness could keep them away from school.

At the end of each unit, the teacher fills in an evaluation form on the activity. Typical questions are: Was student interest maintained throughout the unit? Was the activity at too high (or too low) a level for most students? and What improvement could be made in the unit?

Of equal concern is the question: Are the students learning anything? "Tests at the end of the school year showed that many children in the program had gained a year plus six months." Peery says. "And not one had failed to advance by at least a year."

Months before the tests were made on their children, most parents—even those who at first had disapproved of the new way of teaching—were heartily in accord with the program, although it had not always been easy to get a fair trial for it. "When they complained, we invited them to come to school and watch," Megow says, "If they couldn't come, we went to see them. We asked them to be patient with us for a few weeks, just to let us show them what we were trying to do. Before long we were getting calls from pleased mothers, telling us about children who were doing homework for the first time, because if they didn't they would not be eligible for the next day's project or field trip."

A sixth-grade class at Lovell, classified previously as low achievers, recently finished a unit on hotel-motel management.

They built a four-foot-high cardboard model of a motel right to its balconies, swimming pool, grounds, and surrounding palms. Then they were taken to one of the motels in the area where they talked with managers, maintenance men, and maids. They played roles of guests, hosts, and workers. They telephoned for reservations which were filled by role-playing desk clerks. They figured rates per day, salaries, and labor costs.

At a school assembly student committee chairmen of the project gave a comprehensive report on what they had learned. Weeks later they were happy to repeat their performance for classroom visitors. "Those particular children never would have stood up and talked before. It was a change that came from them getting involved with the careers program," Peery says.

At Wheatley School a unit on land transportation written by Eleanor Jennings for the second through sixth grades covers shipping by truck and freight car. Children learn language arts by reporting on products that are shipped, where they originate, and their use. The youngsters also study vocabulary charts with such special terms as bill of lading, tractor-trailer, switch engine, and so forth. And they learn the various responsibilities of all the people involved by role playing as truck drivers, railroad workers, shipping clerks, warehousemen, and dispatchers.

When they study math, they compute mileage and distance, fuel costs, load weights, wages and hours. In social studies they learn to read maps, and get some idea of the safety requirements, legal restructions, and pollution problems that are all part of moving goods over land. And what better way for youngsters to study science in a meaningful context? They learn about converting the energy of steam or gasoline and air into motion. They study rock strata and road composition and the effects of heat and cold on road surfaces. They see the need for refrigeration and learn principles involved in it."

Art too adds its own special dimension to the subject. The class draws murals of people in shipping operations. Through folk songs and records of truckers and engineers, gandy dancers come alive and Casey Jones crashes old 97 all over again.

From transportation to law enforcement is only a classroom away. A unit on police work so enthralled youngsters in the fourth, fifth and sixth grades that 84 of them wrote the police chief in nearly Apopka saying they hoped to become policemen and couldn't the recruiting age be made a little lower than 21? The surprised chief visited their classes where he talked with the youngsters. Later he arranged special orientation sessions for them at the police station. Pupils rode in squad cars, toured the jail, sat in the radio room, and had some of the administrative duties explained to them.

Each unit depends in large part on contact with actual workers and preferably in on-the-job situations. For example, a construction boon for central Florida has housing developments mushrooming around some of the schools, while at the same time an expressway is being built within yards of school grounds. Normally, these distractions are considered noisy but probably necessary evils. At Lovell School however, Mrs. Grundish took advantage of the house building and road construction to lead her unit out to observe what was going on. Workmen and foremen were delighted to answer questions; they showed the youngsters how to use tools and machines, and explained the sequence of steps required to put up a house or lay down a roadbed. They even furnished builders' scraps to the children to make models.

On the junior high school level prevocational education becomes more complex. Specialists visit the schools, field trips continue, book and reference material become more sophisticated, and career classes flourish. Ninth-grade students at Union Park used election year news as a springboard for studying current politics and researching political history. Hospital and health and careers caught the attention of eighth-grade students. Two seventh-graders produced a creditable 30-minute show on closed-circuit TV at the end of a unit on broadcasting.

"Students who were bored with school are finding it has something for them." says John Daniels, career development specialist at Union.

"Our discipline problems have just about vanished."

Back at Wymore, where the entire faculty and student body is involved in the program, real job training begins. Still it is accomplished in company with academic subjects.

"I am often asked if our students miss out in the humanities area," says Patricia Arredondo, a senior high school curriculum writer. "As a literature major, I too was bothered about that question when I joined the project. Now I can answer honestly and say I don't think they lose as much as they gain. You would be amazed at the broad interest students develop around such practical courses as business law, and the taste they acquire for the study of psychology sometimes begins with the beginning unit for day care aides. There's a supplemental package, too, for those especially interested in academics. Many of these students will go to college after working awhile to pay their way. I know, if I hadn't been able to type I never would have made it."

At Wymore each ninth-grade student selects a career, but any student is free to change later if he or she wants to. Meanwhile courses are open-ended, progressive from level to level, equipping the student for employment even if he should have to drop out after completing the first year of training.

After a year—or less time if one is able and eager—a student who has chosen a career in electrical services, for instance, may receive a certificate showing that he is qualified to repair small resistive appliances such as toasters in the event he must leave school, or for summer employment. Each succeeding year he is trained for a job requiring greater skills and more knowledge. After completing four years training, accomplished at his own pace, the student is certified for trained for a job requiring greater skills and more knowledge. After completing four years training, accomplished at his own pace, the student is certified for major residential, commercial, or industrial work or to enter a technicological college. He is also prepared for the entrance examination required of all students enrolling in Florida's state colleges and universities.

Megow believes everyone, whether he plans to be a mechanic, a composer, or a brain surgeon, should have an immediately employable skill. But his greatest concern is for the 30 percent of American students who drop out before finishing high school and who, without a salable skill, join the cycle of poverty, hopelessness, and crime.

"The program at Wymore is not for everyone," Megow admits, and he's thinking of the person with perhaps business executive ambitions and the means to go through the Harvard Graduate School of Business Administration, for example. In the earlier school years, however, he feels it can help children of all economic backgrounds. "Our aim in the elementary and junior high schools is to make pupils aware of the interest and variety they will find in the grownup world," he says. "To give them a feeling of the dignity of work—any work."

It will take at least ten years to make a complete evaluation of the Orange County Career Development Program, for not until then will the children now in the early grades—the "awareness" phase of career development—be old enough to serve as statistical proof. For the present, the program's success can be inferred only from the enthusiasm of students, teachers, and the majority of the parents, which, incidentally, is not at all a necessarily unreliable gauge.

Dennis T. Torp

CAREER EDUCATION AND THE EXISTING CURRICULUM*

During the late 1960s and early 1970s it became apparent that the existing educational system was limited in providing for the needs of the majority of the students it served. Many high-school students were prepared to enter college for additional education but only a small percentage were prepared to pursue their occupational desires.

It was assumed that in vocational courses a student would acquire the attitudes, self-realization, aspirations, and skills necessary for intelligent decision-making concerning his occupational choice and preparation. But actually, 70 to 80 percent of the secondary curriculum, teaching talent, and resources were, and are, directed at the small percentage of students who require postsecondary educational training.

Paradoxically, when educators are confronted with the question of unemployable people, they respond, "They need more education." The answer lies not with *more* education, but with the *type* of education a student receives.

Career Education Thrust

The term career education thrust describes an educational method whose goals encompass the highest priority society places on a student: his or her career. This method uses the commonalities in existing education, inserts career orientation as a major goal in every subject taught, and provides more personal experiences from which students can make career choices. The goal is to broaden a student's awareness of the job classifications offered in an occupational field, and the education and/or skills required for each.

The problem of including career education in an educational philosophy at the operational level is complicated by lack of teacher preparation to handle a curriculum in which every subject includes career orientation. Another problem

*Dennis T. Torp–"Career Education and the Existing Curriculum" reprinted by permission from the April, 1973 issue of *School Shop* copywright © 1973 by Prakken Publications, Inc.

is that many educators perceive career education as a "new course" which some-how must be inserted into an already overcrowded curriculum. How then can the career education thrust find its place in the educational process?

Career education is a process, not another course. It is an orderly system designed to produce a measurable result. It is a reality-directed attitude to be included as one of the major goals of K-12 education. As a system, it contains components essential to its productivity. One of these is the existing curriculum in the local school district. A subcomponent of the curriculum is the courses included. In preparing to implement the model career education thrust, the first consideration must be the existing curriculum.

To suggest that the career education thrust replace what presently exists is foolish. It should be implemented within the framework of the existing curricu-lum and staff. Three years of operational research, in-service, and implementa-tion have been conducted—with progressive modifications—by the Warren, Michigan, Consolidated Schools. As a result, implementation of a systematic approach for introducing the career education thrust into the existing cur-riculum has emerged. We strongly recommend that this implementation be divided into three or more phases covering a three-year period.

Three-Phase Approach

Phase I

1. Identification of the district educational plan by levels.
2. Isolation of each level and identification of the subject curriculum.
3. Identification of the major and minor learning components utilized in the teaching presentation.
4. Grouping of similarities in subject content by their relationship to career possibilities.
5. Subgrouping of courses utilizing similar effective learning components.
6. Listing of career possibilities which utilize the nature of the course content.
7. Identification of the content, concept, and principles taught in a course as they apply to the world of work.
8. Inclusion of a career-oriented goal within the existing goals of each course.
9. Development of units of study in every course for a limited number of occupational clusters.

Phase II

1. Limit implementation in building where teacher participants in Phase I are regularly assigned.
2. Utilization of units of study developed in Phase I.
3. In-service of other teachers in the building by program participant teachers.

4. Expansion of in-service for teacher by subject conducted by program-participant teacher of the same subject or area.
5. Revision and expansion of units of study.

Phase III

1. Expansion of program to a building at all levels for all subjects or programs.
2. Employment of full-time career education staff, consisting of a director or leader and an elementary and a secondary career education curriculum specialist.

The Galaxy Approach

The career education thrust model was applied to the existing junior-high curriculum, and is in operation in most subjects presently being taught. As this concept gains momentum, support, and acceptance from the administration, staff, and students, new revisions are being proposed for the curriculum, including more career education influence.

One of the junior-high curriculum components which lent itself to the concepts of the career education thrust was the existing Galaxy approach in the Warren Consolidated Schools. Clustering thousands of related job fields by knowledge, manipulative skills, principles, and products made it possible to produce an exploratory experience simulating the major facets of these numerous occupations. These broad groupings or similarities from the various job possibilities produced families or occupational clusters.

Students are exposed to various occupational opportunities through exploratory, manipulative-centered experiences. These experiences are further explored using a limited problem-solving/decision-making approach.

The Galaxy model (see below) indicates the nature of the occupational cluster grouping and typical content being covered.

The career education thrust begins in the elementary grades, K-6, where curriculum emphasis is on awareness, and the major effective learning components deal with attitudes and values. The exploratory curriculum is emphasized at the junior-high-school level, grades 7-9, in which manipulative skills are stressed. The technical theme is the focal point at the high-school level where the goal is a salable skill upon graduation.

Classroom activity centers around the manipulative learning component as an exploratory experience, rather than the task/skill aspect so commonly used. This broad-based actual experience exposure is preferred over the simulated experience as a more reliable criterion for the selection of high-school courses by students. Regardless of the subject content being taught, career education should be included as a major goal of that subject. In planning the content, the teacher

Galaxy Approach

Materials & Processes	*Art*	*Visual Communications*
Woods	2 Dimensional/	Drafting
Hot Metals	3 Dimensional	Printing
Cold Metals	Design/Media	Photography
Machined Metals	Commercial Art	Photocopy
Plastics		
Welding		
Ceramics		
Business	*Energy & Propulsion*	*Personal Services*
Clerk Typist	Electricity	Child Care
Accounting	Electronics	Clothing
Retailing	Internal	Health Occupations
Data Processing	Combustion	Cosmetology
		Consumer Education
		Foods
		Home Management

should include a major emphasis on one of the effective learning components and minor emphasis on the other two. In this way, special occupational clusters such as the communications industry are covered in each subject simultaneously, from the viewpoint of that subject's content.

It is unrealistic to expect a student to select and prepare himself for his occupational interest when he has had only limited exposure to what is available; furthermore, he cannot be expected to prepare to meet the educational or skill requirements if he must gain actual experience after high school. It is the job of education to provide an educational system which presents these experiences as a part of its overall goal.

Robin Pierce

CAREERS ON
THE COMPUTER*

"HELLO, PLEASE ENTER A PERIOD, THEN ENTER YOUR FIRST AND
LAST NAME."

It is late afternoon in the Career Information Center of Winston Churchill High
School in Eugene, Oregon. A boy in blue jeans and a matching denim jacket
leans forward over a noisily rackity-tacking computer teletypewriter terminal.
He reads its message on the yellow paper jutting from the machine. Then he
slowly types in his name with a searching index finger. "J-E-R-R-Y
A-T-K-I-N-S."

There is a few seconds pause. Then the tele-typewriter begins its racing staccato noise again. Rackity tackity tak. The type-wheel flies back and forth beneath the clear plastic shield of the machine. Jerry follows the wheel with his
eyes as it prints out the computer's message, his head moving from side to side as
if he were watching a tennis game in slow motion. "HELLO JERRY. DO YOU
WANT INFORMATION (INFO) ABOUT A PARTICULAR OCCUPATION
NOW, OR WOULD YOU LIKE TO START THE QUESTIONAIRE (QUEST)?
TYPE IN 'INFO' OR 'QUEST.' "

Jerry types in "QUEST."

Again there is a slight pause as the computer digests his message. Then the
staccato noise: "WE WILL NOW BEGIN."

What is Jerry—a boy who gives the impression that he would be more at home
tinkering with an automobile engine than seated before a teletype—doing here?
Why is he so intently reading the computer's message? The answers to these
questions have generated considerable interest among Lane County educators.
They say they have developed a career-information delivery system so appealing
to students that they seek it out voluntarily. Not only that—they *read* what it
has to offer. Any counselor or teacher who has tried to motivate students to
read career information in books can understand the educators' enthusiasm.

Called OIAS (Occupational Information Access System), the new approach
involves a communications network originally designed for administrative
record-keeping by which teletypewriters in each of 40 Lane County junior and

*Robin Pierce—"Careers on the Computer" reprinted with permission from the August/
September, 1972 issue of *American Education,* a publication of the United States Office
of Education, Washington, D.C.

senior high schools are connected by telephone lines to a computer in Eugene. Now the computer has been given the additional job of storing OIAS data. Students find the process of retrieving occupational information from the computer by teletypewriter so fascinating that they willingly stand in line for their turn at the keyboard.

School counselors are still free to guide students to such traditional sources of career information as brochures and books, but they have increasingly become less inclined to do so. For one thing, they say, students rarely read these printed materials, particularly the slow readers for whom the printed page is overwhelming. For another, printed matter cannot handily be updated. And for still another, books and brochures usually present the national picture, whereas most students remain in their home areas to work and thus also need information about the local job situation.

In 1969, Bruce McKinlay, a labor economist at the University of Oregon, became director of a project funded by the Manpower Administration of the Department of Labor to design a career information system that would overcome these problems. The result was OIAS—a system which aims at providing students with continuously updated and localized occupational information in a manner more enticing than books.

Let's return to Jerry Atkins to see how OIAS works.

As his manner correctly suggested, Jerry enjoys exploring beneath the hood of a car. His dream is to acquire an old Model A he can tinker with. At Churchill, he has taken Mechanics 4 and 5, and in his senior year he plans to apply for a mechanics scholarship for training after high school. In addition to thinking of perhaps becoming an auto mechanic, he has also considered the possibilities of truck driving (his father's occupation) or even carpentry or bricklaying or farming. As he says, he would rather work with his hands than at a desk. "Unless, of course, I'm in the army," he quips. "Then a desk would be fine." In any case, he and the OIAS computer are starting to get acquainted.

There are five basic parts to the overall OIAS approach—a questionnaire, occupational descriptions, bibliographies, cassette tapes, and visits with local people. Jerry has used the questionnaire four or five times now, "I like it," he says. "It gets down to the basic questions. A couple of times I've tried it out by answering the questions differently, to see what different lists I get."

The OIAS questionnaire is designed to help the student pinpoint particular occupational areas he might want to explore further. Based on answers to 25 questions, the computer prints out a Quest List—a selection of occupations attuned to his particular abilities and interests. The first time Jerry used the questionnaire, he was surprised to find that "auto mechanic" was left off his Quest List. "So I asked the computer, 'Why not auto mechanic?' It told me that the monthly wage I had put down—$1,000—didn't fit that occupation. I went back and changed my answer to $700, and auto mechanic was on my new list."

Let's follow Jerry through the OIAS procedure better to understand what took place. Before starting a dialog with the computer by typing "HELLO,"

Jerry has circled on a printed questionnaire the answers to 25 questions. As the computer prints out abbreviated forms of these questions, Jerry types in the answers he has circled.

The first question has to do with lifting. "Could you do medium or heavy work? That means a job requiring you to lift 50 pounds or often lift and carry 25-pound objects. . . ." Jerry types in "YES."

Rackity tackity tak. The teletypewriter continues typing out questions. Questions two and three deal with seeing and hearing disabilities, and question four asks Jerry his geographical preferences. There follow questions bearing on such matters as whether he would prefer to work in jobs mainly filled by men, or mainly filled by women, or does not care: on how much training he is willing to undertake; and on his interests and apptitudes in working with people, information, and things.

Jerry has begun the questionnaire with a potential of 210 occupations on his Quest List, a number that includes 95 percent of the job listings in Lane County. As he sets forth more and more of his requirements and preferences, his list is narrowed down. At any point in his conversation with the computer he can type "HOW MANY?" and receive a notation of the number of occupations that have survived his specifications and, if he chooses, a printout list of them. On this occasion Jerry asks, "HOW MANY?" after question 24 and is told by the machine that 88 occupations remain on his list.

He then moves to question 25, which refers to monthly wage requirements: How much must you make (for full-time work) before you would consider working in a job field?" Jerry answers $500. Following this final question the teletypewriter automatically begins reeling off a student's Quest List. Jerry watches as it prints: "THERE ARE 073 OCCUPATIONS THAT CORRESPOND TO THE ANSWERS YOU GAVE." So, as Jerry notes, by his response to question 25 he reduced his options by 15 occupations.

The computer continues: "QUEST LIST FOR JERRY ATKINS: HOTEL & MOTEL MANAGERS . . . RAIL-ROAD CLERKS . . . FLOOR LAYERS . . . VENEER DRYING OCCUPATIONS . . . COMMERCIAL ARTISTS AND DESIGNERS. . ." Jerry closely follows the emerging list.

Seventy-three occupations take a while to print out, leaving a handy interval during which to learn how OIAS has been faring at Churchill High since its installation there in January of 1971. By the following May, with no particular pushing or promotion by the staff, more than half of Churchill's 1,040 students had taken their turn at the keyboard and most had returned to query the computer further. A sampling of parents showed that 64 percent of the students who had conversed with the computer had told their parents about the experience, many even bringing home the yellow printout papers to show off. By now it would appear that OIAS has been used at least once by every student attending Churchill.

Another study showed that 70 percent of the students who used OIAS felt the system had opened their eyes to occupations they would seriously want to consider further. In an ancillary test of knowledge about their career fields, students who had used the OIAS system consistently displayed a greater knowledge about job qualifications than those who had not.

Wayne Hill, a counselor at Churchill, is one of OIAS's most enthusiastic backers. "It's a real godsend," he says, and he recalls a typical incident from pre-OIAS days when he was talking with a student and asked what kinds of careers the youngster was considering. The conversation, he says, went about like this:

Hill: What kind of work do you think you'd be most interested in?

Student: Oh, I dunno.

Hill: Well, what do you like to do?

Student: A little bit of everything, I guess.

Hill: Well is there anything you don't like to do?

Student: No, I like to do most things.

"There just wasn't anything flowing from that youngster," exclaims Hill. "I felt frustrated, and ineffective, and I could hardly keep from shouting, 'Say something! You're not a lump of clay.' "

With the machine the student cannot escape expressing himself in specific, concrete terms, and in the process he can hardly help but develop a feel for the kinds of job opportunities that exist and the responsibilities and requirements they entail. The counselor can in turn capitalize on that newly acquired background by using it as the starting point for productive discussions. "Students have to have good information if they are to make valid career decisions," Hill notes, "and before OIAS they didn't have it."

Hill says a further value of the OIAS process is that it confronts students with the consequences of their choices. "Young people often depend on a gut reaction when it comes to choosing jobs. They say, 'Oh, I just want the job that pays the most money.' If *I* challenge them, they won't listen. But let's say thay are going along on the machine and have narrowed their choices down to 20 jobs. And then they come to the question about the monthly wages they want, and they put down $1,000. That may wipe out all the possible jobs except one. When that happens, they can *see* the implications of their choices."

At Churchill, OIAS is available to students during most of the school day, rather like an unmonitored vending machine. Most other Lane County schools use it more restrictively, often by counselor appointment only. The junior high schools employ the system mainly in a class called "Self Understanding Through Occupational Exploration." In general, Lane County educators feel that the advantages of OIAS are maximized when the system is integrated with counseling programs, career decisionmaking classes, and courses dealing with the development of occupational skills. Wayne Hill uses it in a minicourse called "Careers and Values." Yet he thinks it important to make the system available on an open, unsupervised basis as well. "There are some kids," he says, "who aren't going to talk to a counselor, and that's life. For them the impersonality of the machine is an important factor."

And now it's time to return to Jerry and the printout of his Quest List:
". . . BROADCAST TECHNICIANS . . . WAITRESSES . . . CLERGYMEN . . . FIREMEN . . . RADIO AND TELEVISION ANNOUNCERS." He holds the yellow paper—now three feet long—above the teletype and looks it over. "Hmmm—auto mechanic was left off my list again," he observes. At this point he can make use of one OIAS's most valuable characteristics—its "why not" phase. Jerry can now ask the computer, "WHY NOT 3112?" (The code number for auto mechanic) and learn why it was eliminated from his list. He does so.

"AUTOMOBILE MECHANIC ELIMINATED FROM YOUR LIST BY THE FOLLOWING ANSWERS: ORGANIZING AND USING FACTS 18-NOT" Jerry flips through the questionnaire to question 18 and discovers he had answered that he definitely would not want a job that requires gathering and putting information together and then knowing what to do with it. "I guess auto mechanic would include that," he muses.

The number of occupations on Jerry's Quest List—73—is higher than is usual among high school students. This is because he answered so many questions with "no preference," A more usual (and more preferable) range is from five to 15. If the number is greater than that, a counselor advises the student to go back and answer the 25 questions more restrictively; if the student has less than five, the counselor suggests he be less particular.

Jerry now looks at his Quest List to see if there are any occupations on it that might interest him. Available from the computer are 210 occupational descriptions of about 250 words each, and Jerry can request any of them, regardless of whether or not they appear on his Quest List. In fact, he can skip the questionnaire entirely and go straight to the occupational descriptions, which he often does. He likes to drop into the center occasionally and get a description of an occupation that happens to appeal to him that day. He runs his finger down his Quest List to "9426 FIREMEN." He types in the code number.

Rackity tackity tak. The type wheel races back and forth. "FIREMEN PROTECT COMMUNITIES AGAINST THE LOSS OF LIFE, INJURY, AND DESTRUCTION OF PROPERTY BY FIRE. FIREMEN WORK AS A TEAM WITH EACH MAN ASSIGNED A SPECIFIC JOB . . ."

Jerry grimaces as he reads that firemen "ADMINISTER FIRST AID."

"I'd scratch on that," he says, "I don't like the sight of blood."

After the computer has outlined the tasks of firemen, it prints a paragraph on "CURRENT LOCAL EMPLOYMENT: 175, ALL MALES BETWEEN 22-54." This section also provides a description of the work environment, the work week, and the salary. Then come paragraphs that go into the necessary aptitudes and attitudes, describe the employment outlook, and identify special training needed and where that training is offered. As the teletype continues to print, Jerry reads the words intently. He notes that a two-year program is available at Lane Community College.

Jerry will tell you that he doesn't like to read. He gets little meaning out of books, he says, and declines to keep trying. Yet here he is reading the occupational description of firemen with real enthusiasm. Lane County educators regard this strange ability of the teletype to induce students to read as being one of OIAS's most exciting (and unexpected) side effects. The clatter of the machine and the sense of immediacy it imparts seem to exert a kind of hypnosis—the students just cannot take their eyes off those words. It has been discovered that even the so-called "nonreaders" not only read the material avidly but understand and absorb it. One remedial reading teacher says that the teletype printout is probably the best teaching device she has encountered.

Once again leaving Jerry to the rackity-tacking teletype, let's turn for a moment to some of the nuts and bolts of the OIAS operation. The annual cost of the Lane County system ranges between $1.50 and $2.00 per student. Bill Manley, Career Education Coordinator of Lane Intermediate Education District (the service agency that administers OIAS), says a study has revealed that doing the same job now being performed by OIAS would require two full-time counselors at four times the cost. Even then, he notes, the counselors could not store as much information as the computer, convey it as quickly, or relate it as effectively to the students' individual needs and likes.

Costs to other school districts setting up such a system would doubtless vary widely, depending on such factors as the availability and location of the computer and teletypewriters, the number of components used and the number of persons using the system. In any case, the program can be run on any size computer that can support a teleprocessing network. Since no additional staff is needed to operate the system, it can be used in small schools as well as large.

Updating the labor market information stored in such a system is simple and accomplished by feeding the computer via the teletypewriter. In OIAS this job is performed under a continuing contract with the Career Information System, a statewide cooperative headquartered at the University of Oregon.

And now back to Jerry Atkins. The job description for firemen has ended. The computer next directs Jerry to three other types of related information available in the OIAS program—a selected bibliography of books readily available at the school, a cassette containing recorded interviews with men now working as firemen, and directions for making contact with a local fire marshall for a personal interview.

Jerry rises. He rips off the yellow paper. Maybe another day he will return for a rundown of what's involved in being a carpenter. Or a cabinetmaker. Or any number of other occupations Jerry might consider as he tackles the puzzle of identifying a job clearly fitted to his interests and abilities and aspirations. As he walks out of the Career Information Center, he rolls up the yellow paper and stuffs it away in the pocket of his jeans.

Nolan Estes

THE SKYLINE'S
THE LIMIT
IN DALLAS*

How can a public school district offer its high school students not just a chance to earn a diploma, but also the opportunity to qualify for good jobs after graduation—especially students who have no plans to go on to college?

We're talking now, about jobs that pay today at least $10,000 a year—and commensurately more in the future as the cost of living in America continues to rise.

We know right now that the job market is tight. Yet the need for young people with vocational skills is obviously great. To provide the right training for these jobs at the high school level is a complex procedure, requiring excellent teachers, expensive equipment, and hard-working students.

Another complicating factor is that many students in high school have no long-term vocational plans. Many have only a vague idea of what they want in a job after graduation. Still others are unaware of the natural skills they possess—skills they can develop in school and transfer to jobs after graduation.

Can any high school program meet these obvious, legitimate needs?

The answer is "yes," we think, in Dallas, Texas, where the Skyline Career Development Center, a $21 million facility administered by the Independent School District, today provides students with a comprehensive approach to secondary education. The Skyline program offers not only a traditional high school curriculum but also specialized instruction that helps young people prepare in advance to earn a living in the future.

Take the aviation technology cluster at Skyline as an example. Aviation is one of twenty-eight different career fields that the Center now makes available to its students for study.

Recently licensed by the Federal Aviation Administration to teach a 1,150-hour course in airframe technology, Skyline is putting its license to good use. A graduate of the program can earn as much as $12,000 a year as a licensed airframe technician once he has two years of experience.

---

*Dr. Nolan Estes—"The Skyline's the Limit in Dallas" reprinted with permission from the *PTA Magazine,* June, 1973.

Sidney P. Marland, Jr., Assistant Secretary of Education in the U.S. Department of Health, Education, and Welfare, recently described Skyline as "a model for the nation" in career education. According to Dr. Marland, the Center is not only one of the largest but also one of the most comprehensive secondary education facilities in the country.

Big it is. Located on an 80-acre campus, sprawling Skyline occupies 650,000 square feet of air-conditioned space. It's packed with more than $5 million worth of technological and scientific equipment.

There are three educational components in this multipurpose facility: the career development center; a comprehensive high school for students who live within the attendance zone; and a center for community services.

There is a $1 million computer, a 30,000-square-foot airplane hangar, a color television studio, and a greenhouse for horticultural study—all part of the practical "laboratory" at Skyline in which students can put to work the theories they learn in the classroom.

While study at the Center provides students with marketable skills upon graduation, it also prepares them to attend college. It's up to the graduate to decide which path he will take.

Skyline is a collection of clusters of closely related interests. Each cluster encompasses several "families" of careers, which, in turn, are composed of many specific career options.

For example, one student in the music cluster might want to become a piano tuner, another a professional musician, still another a salesman in a music store. The student planning on going to college can use his Skyline training in the music cluster as an intensive preparation for his major field of study, leading perhaps to a career in music as a teacher, composer, conductor, or critic.

Educational experiences at the Center cut across cluster lines. For example, recently a group of students followed through on every step of the planning and construction of two houses valued at $35,000 each.

A number of clusters within the Center were necessarily involved in the building of the houses, beginning with the architectural plans and continuing through the various phases of carpentry, plumbing, electrical work, decorating, air conditioning, and landscaping. The students also produced a sales brochure for the houses when they were completed.

As the houses went up, students from other clusters—environmental control systems, interior design, architectural careers, horticulture, visual arts, graphics communication, and photographic arts—contributed their specialized skills. The result? The houses were built, and the students gained valuable "real" experience building them.

A student at Skyline usually finds out early in life if he is really as interested in a certain career field as he thinks he is. The student who discovers in high school that he is preparing himself for the wrong career is better off, obviously, than the student who makes that discovery as a junior in college.

A major factor in the success of the Skyline program has been the involvement of some 275 adults in the Dallas community, people who are leaders in business, industry, and education. These men and women serve on the Skyline advisory board and other advisory committees. They bring to Skyline the special expertise of the business community.

One of the advisory board's major interests is to keep the educational experiences at Skyline current with day-to-day developments in business and industry. The members also make sure that the Center remains responsive to actual needs in the community.

Advisory board members also assist curriculum committees in setting up courses, obtain needed equipment, and remove obstructions that might prevent classes from getting underway. They arrange field trips, serve as guest lecturers, and help to evaluate student progress. Many board members also provide part-time or summer work opportunities for students at Skyline, and later on help graduates find their first full-time job.

A conservative price tag on the help—in terms of time and materials—that the advisory board has given Skyline during the school's first year of operation would be in excess of $150,000.

An important facet of the Skyline program is its coordination of curriculum with programs offered at Dallas County Community College, where advanced study opportunities are available in each of the career fields offered at Skyline. Students who wish to continue their studies beyond high school can easily do so. Degree programs in each field are also available at a senior college or university.

Although the student body at Skyline includes young people who live within the 350-mile Dallas school district, each spring students from all eighteen high schools in the district can apply for admission for the fall term. Criteria for acceptance include aptitude, interest in the program requested, previous achievements in school, citizenship, and maturity. Free transportation is provided.

The programs at Skyline are nongraded so that each student can proceed at his own pace. He is tested on his work in a course as soon as he completes it, rather than being forced to wait for the entire class to finish.

In place of the standard A, B, C report-card system, the Skyline approach is to assess each student's progress in terms of his performance. On report-card day, the parent gets a print-out of the behavioral objectives the student has completed within the reporting period and a cumulative total of the objectives he has completed during the year.

Not every school district could build or would want to build a Career Development Center like the one at Skyline. But districts that *are* interested in creating a similar program can learn much from the Dallas experience in career education. Several recommendations for school districts thinking about beginning a "skyline" of their own would include:

1. Advice from the business and industrial community is absolutely essential to plan and operate a realistic school program relevant to the world of work.
2. The program must be "open-entry" and "open-exit." It should allow each

student to progress at his own pace and to choose a direction suitable to his aspirations and abilities.

3. Every student finishing high school should be prepared to exercise the option of going directly into the world of work. He should also, however, be equipped to continue his education in a trade school, junior college, or university should he choose to do so. These options should be available to the student right up to graduation day, rather than be forces in a decision that he must make in grade eight or nine.

4. The high school program should be coordinated with trade schools and other institutions of higher learning so that additional educational opportunities in a particular field will be available to the student after graduation.

5. Programs should be based on performance with criterion-reference testing built into them. These should never jell, however, to the point that continuous improvements cannot be made.

6. Equipment should be updated constantly to match improvements in business and industry.

These factors are reasons why many school people in Dallas believe that the Skyline program has been so enthusiastically accepted by students, parents, industry, and the community itself.

The same factors also help to explain why the Dallas Independent School District now feels that, at long last, it is able to offer students learning experiences as meaningful and exciting as the real world.

The Skyline program *has* made "exciting education" available in Dallas. There's no reason why similar programs—modified in terms of the needs and assets of individual communities—can't make the same kind of "exciting education" available to many more high school students throughout our land. The prospect is certainly worth more than a try.

Marie Y. Martin

ADVANCING
CAREER EDUCATION*

An educator whose responsibilities involve a fair amount of travel in the United States quickly becomes aware that American education is today undergoing a major shift in direction. The potential impact of this phenomenon doubtless will not become fully apparent for many years, but that a fundamental change is occuring there can be no question.

At its core is a new view of education's function. In every section of the country, a significant number of schools and colleges are seeking to reorient and broaden their purposes. Their common goal is to respond to the student's specific, immediate educational needs in a manner that serves his long-term aspirations for a satisfying and meaningful life after his schooling is ended. This is career education, a concept which recognizes that learning is more than an intellectual exercise—that in stretching people's minds and honing their sense of values, the schools and colleges have the further obligation of preparing them to launch successful working careers.

Nowhere is this thesis better illustrated than in our community junior colleges. Careeer education is in fact as current as the newest of these institutions and as old as the first of them. And with the stimulus of The Education Amendments of 1972, the community colleges will be called upon to play an even larger role in spreading the career education concept. From their beginning, the two-year colleges have emphasized programs that are responsive to the needs both of their students and of the society in which those students will live. Given that approach—plus what would appear to be a growing pragmatism among students, a determination to weigh their schooling in terms not of a degree as such but of its application to the job market—it is not to be wondered at that Census Bureau reports show these institutions as accounting for almost all of the increase in college freshman and sophomore enrollments between the years 1966 and 1971. Expectations are that this year the overall community college student body will exceed 2.5 million—something in the order of 30 percent of total undergraduate college enrollments.

Many will of course be in a transfer status that enables them to go on to a four-year college or university. Even among these students, however, there is a

---

*Dr. Marie Y. Martin—"Advancing Career Education" reprinted with permission from the August/September, 1972 issue of *American Education,* a publication of the U.S. Office of Education, Washington, D.C.

sharply increasing trend toward combining transfer programs with occupational courses. The net result is still further stimulus to a revolutionary overhaul of education, evidenced by such developments as the wide departure from standard curriculum, flexible scheduling, the acceptance of work experience for college credit, new approaches to counseling, novel methods of teaching, unconventional types of facilities, the varied background and experience of the faculty, and many others.

Given the current widespread interest, it is surprising how recently career education has emerged as a national movement. The concept clearly touched a vital chord. Its beginnings reach back only to January of 1971, to a speech made by Dr. Sidney P. Marland, Jr. a few weeks after he had been sworn in as the 19th U.S. Commissioner of Education. As Dr. Marland pointed out on that occasion, despite American education's unquestioned accomplishments, it can take little credit for its performance in making sure that no one leaves school unequipped to get and hold a decent job. Just about half our high school students, he said—in the order of 1,500,000 in any given year—are involved in schooling that prepares them neither for careers nor for college. And of the three out of ten high school graduates who go on to higher education, a third will drop out and a depressing proportion of the remainder will emerge with degree in hand but no clear-cut idea in mind of what to do with it.

In subsequent meetings with educators, students, representatives of business and labor, leaders of various professional associations, members of ethnic groups, State and local government officials, and many others, Dr. Marland has continued to urge consideration of the career education concept: "education that prepares one to think and to care about social responsibility and personal intellectual fulfillment, but education that also equips all learners, at whatever age, with satisfying and rewarding competencies for entering the world of work in the field of one's choice."

The climax in establishing career education high on the Nation's agenda came when President Nixon made the concept an important element in his 1972 State of the Union message to Congress and established it as a White House priority. The discussion has by now become nationwide, and so has the move to translate ideas into action. In an increasing number of educational institutions and at various levels of the school experience, career education is proving to be a systematic way of helping students gain an understanding during the course of their academic studies of the many careers available in the United States—something over 20,000—and preparing them for the career of their choice.

The leadership being exerted by the community colleges in exemplifying and strengthening these principles is particularly noteworthy. Hundreds of such institutions in hundreds of localities have initiated programs that merit the study of educational decisionmakers at every level. The character of their innovations and practices can be illustrated by focusing on six of these colleges, located in various parts of the country. The summaries that follow are based on personal observation; extensive interviews with administrators, faculty, and students; and materials supplied by the individual institutions.

Pasadena City College in Pasadena, California, offers no less than 64 career-oriented courses from commercial airline pilot training to metal processes technology. Such courses engage about half of its 14,000 students, with the other half taking transfer courses in preparation for entering four-year colleges. Among Pasadena's instructional staff are many of its own graduates who have gone on to universities, received degrees, worked in various career fields, and now are regular or part-time members of the faculty. As with many community colleges, Pasadena seeks to recruit a faculty that is representative of the makeup of the student body, and it encourages them to reach beyond the college itself and work with other groups in the community.

Typifying the stress placed on interdisciplinary cooperation between the academic and "practical" skills, each year at Pasadena the students build and sell a model home to the highest bidder—enlisting as they do so the interest and cooperation of representatives of the professions, labor, and business. Students studying architecture develop a range of designs, with the best being chosen on a competitive basis. Students in architectural specifications then take over, drawing up the specs and making sure they are followed by the students in construction classes. Students of interior design select the color schemes to be used and decide upon the drapes and furnishings. The printing and lithography students prepare advertisements and brochures. Business classes participate in preparing bid specifications. And helping from the sidelines at every step is an advisory committee composed of practicing architects and experts from the construction unions, trade associations, utility companies, and furniture stores, some of which donate materials for the project.

Pasadena has 71 off-campus educational sites—in churches, schools, parks, vacated factories, and the like—where classes are offered in courses ranging from power sawing to grocery store operations. A key component of this PCC community action program is a mobile career guidance unit. Moved from place to place in low-income neighborhoods, it serves as a center for job aptitudes testing, counseling, and information about subjects available at PCC's main and satellite campuses.

New York City Community College of the City University of New York is located on a small site in Brooklyn and serves an ethnically mixed student body of 8,000 men and 7,000 women in 34 different career education and college transfer courses. About 80 percent of the students have chosen one or more of the career courses, which are offered both day and evening. The overall career program has three components—general education, orientation, and training in specific skills, with the curriculum for the latter being determined largely by the entry level requirements of industry or by the State's licensing boards. Provisions also are made for training in skills and general educatioion requirements needed for advancement in jobs beyond the entry level.

Student needs and industry demands have an important impact on NYCCC's offerings. Located as it is near the center of the advertising industry, for example, the college has developed programs responding to the continuing demand for people trained in commercial art, graphic arts, and advertising technology. New York is also rich in opportunities for graduates in hotel and restaurant management, and chefs from the college hold their own in the face of top competition and frequently start their first job at a salary of $8,000 a year. Of some 150 students participating in cooperative education programs in engineering technologies, data processing, and accounting, better than 80 percent were offered permanent jobs by the companies with whom they had been gaining experience.

Supportive services offered by the college include an aggressive outreach to students who need counseling by experts in specific fields and the establishment of advisory committees which help develop and update programs, arrange for the availability of advanced equipment, and serve as major resources for job placement. In addition, there is a Special Services Tutorial Project funded by the U.S. Office of Education and an Anti-Drug Use Program funded by the State.

Various career programs operated by the college's Office of International Development and Recruitment send increasing numbers of counselors into local high schools, and the Division of Continuing Education sponsors courses at local senior citizens centers. Other community-based programs are provided in low-cost housing complexes, and NYCCC recently has experimented with the idea of offering credit courses at a community church to give adults an opportunity to "try out" college before making a commitment to enroll at the main campus.

Central Piedmont Community College in Charlotte, North Carolina, never closes its doors on the 8,000 students it serves—56 percent of whom are men and 44 percent women. Its instructional program runs around the clock, partly to make full use of expensive facilities and handle heavy class loads, and partly to accommodate students who have jobs during the day. (Thus an automobile mechanics course, for example, gets under way at midnight and runs until 7 a.m.) For these same reasons, Central Piedmont is a year-round institution, and about 70 percent of the students who attend during the regular academic year enroll in summer classes to complete trade and vocational courses.

In all, Central Piedmont offers 34 occupational programs. One of the most recent to be added to the curriculum is a Human Services Associate degree program geared to employment in day care centers, nursing homes, orphanages, and other welfare-related service agencies. President Richard Hagemeyer is particularly proud of the new career education building being constructed in part with support from the Office of Education. "As in every community," he points out, "Charlottes, greatest educational need is in the occupational area—preparation of students for gainful employment."

Moraine Valley Community College, located in the southwest suburbs of Cook County, Illinois, is attended by about 3,800 students, of whom 42 percent are formally enrolled in career education programs, though in fact virtually the entire student body is engaged in some courses relating to careers. The college currently offers 27 programs leading to an Associate degree in applied science or to a one-year certificate. In addition, a number of continuing education classes are provided for people seeking to improve themselves professionally or simply to enrich their lives, and the college sponsors seminars, workshops, and institutes for nearby municipalities, industries, and others.

In an exemplary program in Industrial Engineering Technology devised by MVCC faculty and one of its community consultant committees, each student individually pursues specified measurable objectives organized according to particular job factors. This means that if a student completes only part of the program he will still be qualified for a job in one of the industrial technology fields (though of course at a lower level) because he has mastered at least some of the required skills. The program is organized in such a way as to make it possible for all students to be working on different tasks at the same time and to select among alternative approaches to learning those tasks.

In general, MVCC seeks to reflect the collective educational needs of the community and to exercise leadership in meeting those needs.

Community College of Denver has 7,200 students enrolled on its three campuses, and of them 64.4 percent are participating in career programs. The average age of CCD's students is 27, and 75 percent hold full- or part-time jobs. As a response to this unusual student body, the college has defined career education as education which meets the needs of the individual as determined by the individual himself. Particular help in making the determination is provided by a career center which op rates on the theory that the individual's chance of choosing a satisfying career is directly proportional to the number of occupations he knows about and understands. In developing the informational material necessary to serve that purpose, the center has become a major learning resource not only for the students and faculty but for high school and junior high school counselors and for the community at large.

Recognizing that many students need experiences in many career fields before they can intelligently settle on one, the college allows students to develop schedules that permit them to try out introductory courses in a number of different occupations, moving at any time from one program to another if they find that their initial choice proved unsuitable.

One of the basic elements in CCD's effort to assist individuals with career choices is a group of instructional laboratories covering basic skills. Most instruction is either individualized or carried out with very small groups. Some students enroll in the instructional laboratory and at the same time pursue their career program, while others concentrate on acquiring basic skills before they enter the program.

Lane Community College in Eugene, Oregon, was established to serve as the career education center for the quarter million people living in the State's southern Willamette Valley and its environs. Business, civic, and educational leaders give enthusiastic support to this college, which serves nearly 20,000 full-

and part-time students each year. Lane offers more than 42 separate career-oriented fields, each designed to lead directly to employment at the end of a one- or two-year period of preparation. A lower division transfer curriculum is also offered.

Lane is a place of change, not in its definition of career education but in how that definition is translated into action. Courses are added or deleted to reflect shifts in the job market, and the emphasis of instruction has moved to a concentration on the personal needs of the individual. A key step in achieving that goal has been the development of more than 850 "VIP's"—Vocational Instructional Packages designed by the faculty with the assistance of experts from business, labor, industry, and the professions.

An open-entry/open-exit instructional strategy allows the student to enter a program at any time, accomplish his objectives at his own rate, and exit from the program no sooner and no later than he can meet the requirements of the job he is pursuing. Placement services are provided, and the college maintains constant liaison with the business community and with the Oregon State Employment Office, enabling students to receive up-to-the-minute information about job opportunities and current wage levels. All students receive on-the-job experience before completing their programs, thanks in large part to cooperative arrangements with local firms.

At Lane—and at Pasadena, New York City CC, Central Piedmont, Moraine Valley, and Denver—career education is a vital force. The same can be said of hundreds of others among the more than 1,100 community colleges in the United States and its territories. These institutions have much to offer, not only to their students but to people interested in exploring the career education concept. I am sure that all of them, and particularly the six I have discussed, would welcome your inquiries and would be glad to have you visit them.

John F. Grede

THE ROLE OF COMMUNITY COLLEGES IN CAREER EDUCATION*

Sidney P. Marland, Jr. has made it abundantly clear that elementary and secondary education should be reoriented along career lines.

The role of postsecondary education—particularly the community college—is less clear, both in terms of how it should be reoriented and what role it may play in the reorientation of all education. It may well be that the key to reorienting elementary and secondary education—or for that matter all education—lies with the postsecondary schools and particularly the community college.

Community college people, especially those who see their primary role in Career Education, will raise some questions concerning a statement that Dr. Marland made on January 23, 1971. "All education is Career Education, or should be. And all our efforts as educators must be bent on preparing students either to become properly, usefully employed immediately upon graduation from high school or to go on to further formal education."

If all education is Career Education, why must the high school graduate either be prepared for immediate employment *or* further formal education? Why not for both, particularly if further formal education beyond the high school is Career Education, as all education is, or should be?

Career Preparation Beyond the High School

At least three factors make career preparation beyond the high school level increasingly important. First, many of the "new careers" feature technicians, the paraprofessional or middle-manpower positions in industry, business, health, and government that require training and education beyond the conventional high school level. The national need for technical skills arising from expanding technology is growing at least twice as fast as the need for professional skills. And the programs to prepare these technicians, as well as the professionals, are found largely at postsecondary or higher education levels.

---

*John F. Grede — "The Role of Community Colleges in Career Education" reprinted with permission from *Essays On Career Education, op.cit.*

Second, the high school level of job preparation historically has been closely associated with the term vocational and runs the risk of retaining its low status if left without an effective bridge to higher education. Status may be enhanced by internal improvements in career-oriented education at the high school level. Status may be enhanced even more if such education is not conceived of as an end in itself nor as an alternative to further formal education, but rather as one possible breakout point in a planned system of Career Education that encourages the student to follow to the fullest a career line compatible with his interests, abilities, and placement probabilities.

Third, the higher education component of a system of Career Education is important—perhaps crucial—if for no other reason than that much motivation in the American educational hierarchy derives from the upward social and economic mobility associated with going to college. Although the prestige of higher education is somewhat diminished by the current inability to deliver adequately on the implied promise of jobs, its influence nevertheless so thoroughly permeates the lower levels of education that it cannot be ignored. Furthermore, the public and student concept of the primary mission of the university is that it provides an entree to well-paid and prestigious jobs. Students to to college to further careers. It may take a public confession to bring home the fact that providing "union cards" to better jobs is really what higher education is all about, particularly with the move toward mass public higher education. Finally, higher education is in Career Education, like it or not, since it now includes over 1,000 community colleges with some 750,000 students enrolled in hundreds of different career programs. This can't be brushed aside.

The real issue of the role of higher education in Career Education is not whether it is included—that seems predetermined—but what kind of model will prevail to influence the patterns of Career Education in the entire educational system.

At the risk of oversimplifying, there appear to be two models or systems of Career Education in the American structure. The first might be called *traditional career preparation* as viewed by colleges and universities. The second is the emerging *community college conception*. Traditional career preparation was and still is shaped by higher education and in particular by the professional schools— medicine, law, engineering, social service, library science, accounting, public administration—those with recognized professional standing or those aspiring to such status.

Community College Career Program Structure

The emerging community college career program structure is moving in different directions and operating on different assumptions than traditional professionally oriented career programs do. The community, for example, is much smaller than the statewide, or more often nationwide, community to which the senior institutions respond for recruiting and placement. In this sense, the community college approach is a saturation technique aimed at the entire community of young and old, disadvantaged and mainstream, minorities and "majorities," rather than a selective group of educationally talented youth.

The open-door admissions policy of the community college even expands to a "reach out" policy for uniformed and nontraditional learners who do not find the door and walk in of their own accord. Students generally are admitted to the college with the assumption that a program is available for all types. In theory the student is primary, the program is secondary; it is the function of the institution to provide the program to fit the student rather than to select out and admit only those students who meet the prerequisites of particular programs.

As a result of the concern for students of all kinds, the number of career programs is large. Typical community colleges offer programs in 25 or 30 specialities with a good spread in such clusters as engineering and industrial, business and secretarial, health, personal and social services, and agriculture. In contrast to the big 4-year package "take-it-or-leave-it" approach of the senior institutions, career programs in community colleges are moving toward a modular conception in which job skills and related knowledge may be broken up into small sequences that can be recognized by a certificate and that the student may pyramid one on top of another until he acquires a full 2-year associate degree. At each step he has a floor under him, so that if he cannot or chooses not to go on to the next higher level, he will have a marketable skill and will not have to go back to ground zero.

Early specialization. In contrast to the traditional insistence on broad theoretical and often unfocused exposure to the liberal arts and sciences as a prerequisite to specialized job preparation courses, community college career programs are predicated on early specialization. Career courses, sometimes called "meat courses," which have a direct and obvious connection with a chosen field need to be offered early to attract and hold students. This is particularly true of the community college student, because he characteristically puts one foot in the job market and keeps the other in the educational institution. The associate degree program in nursing, for example, places the young nursing student in white uniform in a hospital situation in the first semester.

From another perspective, early specialization is virtually indigenous to community colleges because of their strong involvement with out-of-school adults who seek upgrading or updating in present jobs or preparation for new jobs. These students come equipped with the maturity and experience to enable the institution to forego much preparatory work and many prerequisites.

Early specialization creates problems for the traditional pyramid of education that assumes a movement from general preparation to specifics. This concern undoubtedly had much more relevance in an era of relatively slow technological change than it does today when it probably is more reasonable to give specific job training the higher priority. Adaptation to changing technology and changing job requirements can be handled adequately by bringing the individual back occasionally for specific upgrading and updating rather than trying to provide him in advance with the broad, general experience that hopefully makes him adaptable to changing conditions.

Blend of general and special education. The emphasis on early specialization calls for a change in the sequence of special and general education, but it does not imply any lessening of the role of general education. Fundamental to the community college is the concept that specialized education for job competancy and general education for personal and social competancy never are as effective alone as they are coupled together.

There are several practical reasons for blending general education with job preparation. It is still true that more jobs are lost through inability to relate effectively to other people than through lack of technical competence. It is also true that the worker who is unwilling to learn to read, write, and speak English effectively cannot realistically come up with an alternative mode of verbal communication. It is also true that increased productivity, resulting from the same modern technology that creates much of the demand for new career positions, provides the potential for more leisure and more cultural and creative experiences to utilize that leisure. Finally, the community colleges have found the historical significance of general education in the accreditation process to be a strong motivating force requiring them to maintain a balance of general and specialized education.

Career lattice. The perceptions of the role of other institutions in the educational hierarchy is probably different for community colleges than for senior institutions. Community colleges increasingly are moving toward the career lattice concpet, a concept that assumes a freedom of movement of students from one level of institution to another with full credit given for the formal education received at the lower level. The career latice concept also assumes a cooperative relationship in program development among the senior institutions, the community colleges, the high schools, and even the military and the proprietary institutions with which an increasing number of contractural relationships are being effected. This concept assumes the kind of progression wherein a high school student, for example, may have been exposed to the health occupations in elementary school and then during his high school career may have taken a short program to become a certified laboratory assistant. His high school work, with or without the supplement of additional work experience, is accepted by the community college, which adds work largely in laboratory sciences, communications skills, and liberal arts and makes him eligible to take his medical laboratory technician examination at the same time that he receives an associate degree. Advantageous military and proprietary school training may be applied here. Then, with or without any employment in his speciality (which he may elect if he wants some realistic experience plus additional income), he may apply to a senior institution that may add additional components, possibly including management techniques and supervised work experience as well as more refined practices in medical laboratory specialities. At the end of this career line he is a full medical technician with a baccalaureate degree. This type of structure assumes that each institution plays a vital and significant role in the total Career Education of the individual. It doesn't assume that any institution has a monopoly, but that all share in providing an effective, accessible, and flexible career line as part of a career lattice. They all share in the recognition and status since they are integral parts of a process producing qualified job-ready people at several points rather than only at the end of the career line.

Nontraditional education. The evolution of the career lattice concept is closely related to the growing practice of establishing academic equivalents for nontraditional, nonformal education as an alternative route to the rewards offered by higher education. This concept is particularly applicable to career-oriented education and experience, even though evaluating instruments still are largely concentrated in the academic areas. The obvious relevance of converting nontraditional education into formal academic equivalents is that it permits shorter career lines and realistically recognizes that individual study, travel, proprietary-school work, military training, and job experience may in fact produce greater career competence than strictly formal schooling.

One additional advantage of the nontraditional educational thrust (as well as the career lattice) is the encouragement offered many students from poverty level homes and minority ethnic groups who see a desirable career goal in the distance but cannot afford to invest in the total process because of the consequent delay in gainful employment. Such students may accept a shorter and less prestigious job preparation program if it, along with subsequent work experience, is convertible into the higher levels of a compatible career line at senior institutions.

Determination of equivalencies for nontraditional experiences, however, is a two-way street. It also will require that formal academic course work be objectified if any dependable comparability is to be attained.

Additional characteristics. The community college model of Career Education holds that guidance and counseling are of paramount importance. In contrast to traditional college programs, the broad scope and relative newness of many community college career programs require that much more assistance be given to students in selecting compatible offerings, since these programs are not as well known or advertised as medicine, law, or engineering. The community college student needs not only more guidance, but more support through academic and personal counseling, tutoring, and financial assistance.

The community college model of Career Education is acquiring a big-city emphasis in serving a realistic cross-section of urban America. This kind of mission requires not just offerings tailored exclusively to senior colleges, but programs ranging from simple job skills and basic literacy all the way through such associate-degree programs as nursing, auto mechanics, midmanagement, and law enforcement. Nor are community college programs confined to campuses. Career-oriented community service programs are reaching physically into the ghettos and barrios with ethnically balanced staffs and liberal programs of financial support.

The heterogeneity of community college programs, appealing to a wide range of abilities and interests, requires an extremely flexible approach to learning with varying instructional styles geared to different learning styles. It means providing, in addition to the traditional lecture and laboratory approaches of senior institutions, such individualized instructional methods as autotutorial, computer-assisted instruction, small seminars, and discussion groups. This individualization of instruction places a heavy demand on precise determination of objectives that can be stated in measurable terms for both courses and programs.

Such behavioral objectives not only provide an efficient base for learning but are absolutely fundamental to the articulation process. Until such time as the objectives of a course and the program of which it is a part can be stated in terms more precise than typical catalog descriptions, and thus can be compared with counterparts in other institutions, it will be almost impossible to build a systematic cross-institutional Career Education system. In the building of such a system, the community college may take the lead.

The community college so far has conceived of itself as unique. Now, however, it needs to concern itself with its role in a system of career-oriented education, not only as an integral part of the system, but as a change agent to bring about that system. The extent to which the community college model will prevail and influence Career Education and the extent to which it will help bring about a coordinated and cooperative system of Career Education depends on several factors.

Advantages of the Community College Model

Perhaps the most important factor in determining the influence of the community college on Career Education is the extent to which the community college makes good on its promise. It is an ideal vehicle and model for Career Education in the current mode, since it embraces education for job competence, along with social and personal competence. It represents democracy in higher education in that it gives a full range of career choices for young people, working people, and particularly minority groups. Its programs are aimed at the manpower areas of greatest promise for present and future employment. Its immediate target is roughly three-quarters of the employment spectrum, including the semi-skilled, skilled, technical, and middle-management areas while traditional baccalaureate programs aim at one-quarter It is a relatively new and flexible institution with a changing mission. Its recent big-city thrust brings it closer to the problems of urban living, many of which are closely associated with job skills and literacy. Finally, its intermediate position between the high school and senior institutions makes it the logical linking pin in the planning and development of a network of career programs.

Concerns About the Community College

There are concerns, however. On a broad national basis the proportion of community college students in career programs is only 30 percent. The programs are still weighted toward the older business and industrial clusters, although they are moving toward the more marketable health and public service occupations. Two-year degrees still are the norm, although there is increasing interest in shorter, more flexible certificate programs that really provide basic elements in a career lattice structure. Output and placement in relation to student input in career programs is still unimpressive. Many colleges still need to go back to fundamentals such as the careful selection of career programs geared not only to student interests and abilities but to local and national manpower needs.

Some colleges need to establish closer working relationships with business, industry, and public employers for advisory services, work experience, and even instructional assistance. All need to provide effective job placement and followup and to gather institutional data on output and cost so that these data can be fed back into the process to improve effectiveness.

Older junior colleges face internal resistance as they move from an emphasis on individual courses geared to senior institutions toward self-contained, sequenced programs deeply influenced by non-academicians. Career programs need to be developed for real job requirements rather than be warmed-over versions of traditional courses and curriculums developed for senior college requirements. The very organization of teaching needs to relate more closely to programs, so that an educational unit is not just faculty grouped in a similar discipline but a composite of faculty, students, and program fused together toward completion and placement.

Career Education requires adequate administrative support. It requires a student personnel service sympathetic to, and well informed about, career programs, with a willingness to accept a major role in matching students and programs, monitoring their progress, and when necessary, effecting changes. It requires an accurate determination of costs so that a sensible groundwork is provided for program initiation, continuance, modification, or elimination.

To date great progress has been made in community college career programs, commonly without much cooperative effort with either senior institutions or high schools. For that cooperative effort to develop, for the community college to assume a wider role as a potential keystone in the arch of comprehensive Career Education, the community college must make good on its own model. Further, the implication of that model must be known and accepted by a wide audience.

Implications for Other Institutions

The first implication is that of alternative routes to the highest career level. The traditional route has been the straight-line school route to the top, with the high school and junior college each playing a predetermined and accredited role preparatory to the professional schools.

The second route includes a longer but probably more secure and more realistic preparation through a blend of school and related work, with credit given for nontraditional experience and with modular structure for certain marketable breakout points.

For example, the elementary school might provide orientation to the general health fields. The young person then might choose to prepare to be a nurse aide while obtaining a high school diploma, then choose to work in this specialty while earning an associate degree program in nursing at the nearby community college. On passing the registry exam, he or she might accept a position in a hospital or nursing home and begin a baccalaureate program for nurses that provides full acceptance of the associate-degree training and work experience in a telescoped and more specialized baccalaureate program. The combination of training and experience might permit functioning as a physician's assistant. The ultimate career goal might be to become a medical doctor.

This second, or alternative, route provides distinct advantages. The individual who can't afford to study for 6 to 8 years consecutively to go through the straight-line progression of the professional school has an alternative of gainful employment that also provides practical training experience toward an ultimate career goal. Then too, the loss of skilled manpower to society and the psychological shock to individuals who cannot make it all the way is minimized in that an individual may halt his own career line voluntarily and with dignity at the appropriate breakout points.

A second implication of the community college career model is that specialization and generalization may occur in different sequences and may even occur simultaneously. Specialization or generalization is not the monopoly of any educational level. The primary objective is to develop job skills simultaneously with general education so that an individual has a marketable "cluster" wherever he is on the career line.

A third implication of the community college model is that of cooperative articulation. For many years the junior colleges have made overtures to the senior institutions to get more flexible admissions policies. In the last 2 years the City Colleges of Chicago and community colleges in Illinois have been approached by the senior institutions—particularly by the two new upper-division institutions—with the objective in mind of jointly planning developing senior institutional career-oriented capstone programs on top of community college career programs. This kind of effort virtually means joint acceptance of students with full credit awarded for community college courses in the jointly planned program.

In such a truly cooperative endeavor, courses and programs at all levels are virtually subject to public scrutiny. This is a far cry from the selective process accompanying control of programs by single institutions or by particular faculty members of a single institution.

The obvious objective of an effective Career Education system embracing the three implications cited earlier is a total career lattice with the elements in the system identified and with possible pathways marked clearly. The major elements of a career lattice in Illinois, for example, exist in three major strata: the professional schools in the senior institutions; the technical or occupational programs in the community colleges; and the range of vocational programs offered in general high schools, vocational high schools, and secondary-area vocational institutions. The current structure suffers in that the lattice is incomplete. No counterparts for some of the occupational programs that have been developing in the community colleges exist in senior institutions and vice versa. Only recently, for example, have 4-year institutions developed data processing programs. Law enforcement and environmental science specialties at the community college still find few 4-year programs matched to them. Conversely, the field of medicine has not developed a program at the community college level leading to the M.D. degree. Perhaps the physician's assistant program will remedy this. The law graduate has no counterpart in the 2-year programs, although the legal assistant or the legal aide program researched by the American Bar Association has been introduced in a few community colleges.

Perhaps more important than the development of counterparts is the need for the general public and the student to recognize the interrelationships that now exist or that might be effected among programs at various educational levels. Preferably, this identification of interrelationships should include the not-for-profit and proprietary institutions.

This lack of identification indicates that organization and coordination across institutional lines is overdue. The obvious need is to reduce fragmentation resulting from lack of coordination and to eliminate gaps as well as unnecessary duplication. The critical issue is how to do it.

It may well be that legislators are more cognizant of the fragmentation that characterizes the Career Education structure than are educators and are more willing to do something about it.

The public and legislative concern and frustration at the fragmentation of the American educational system, insofar as Career Education is concerned, is expressed in the Higher Education Amendments of 1972. Title X of the Amendments speaks most specifically to the issue. Prophetically, it brackets the community college, occupational education, and adult education into one omnibus section. It provides for new structures—a new bureau to be exact—that will recognize occupational education *per se*. The fact that occupational or Career Education is an integral part of the Amendments that tie together previous legislation for higher education seems to place much emphasis on the role of higher education, and particularly the community college, in occupational education. The provision for a State Commission with a Community College Advisory Group mandated to work with it seems to bespeak congressional intent for broad-based planning that will provide a rational and well-articulated structure for Career Education involving all levels.

Summary

In summary, then, the community college needs to make good on its own promises and to improve its own substance and posture in relation to Career Education. At the same time, it needs to export its concepts of educational programs for all people, of universal access to Career Education at all levels, and of a promise of success at one or more of these levels. Such education needs to be concerned not only with individual differences in ability, interest, financial resources, and ethnic origin, but with manpower needs for a technologically oriented society.

To date the community college has looked inward. It now needs to look toward the other institutions with which a cooperative system of career programs can be developed and implemented. Such a system hopefully could use community college concepts as a base from which to modify and strengthen its structure. Central to such an effort is the career lattice concept from which derives the need for alternate routes to a career goal, for a measureably effective combination and sequence of job skills and general education, and for a continuing cooperative approach to articulation.

The catalyst for a more comprehensive, coordinated, flexible, economic, prestigious, productive, and publicized system of Career Education may be the community college. In keeping with its past history, the community college will take this role in stride.

PART 3

Career Clusters

In a question and answer article in *American Education*, November, 1971, Sidney P. Marland, suggested that within a given school system, Career Education would have to be approached from two basic aspects, curriculum and career interest.

Experts have identified some 20,000 different kinds of jobs. U.S.O.E. has determined that these jobs can be grouped within fifteen general clusters.

Agri-Business and Natural Resources
Business and Office
Communications and Media
Construction
Consumer and Homemaking
Environment
Fine Arts and Humanities
Health
Leisure (Recreation, Hospitality, & Tourism)
Manufacturing
Marine Science
Marketing and Distribution
Personal Services
Public Service
Transportation

Marland suggests that "During the first six years of his schooling the youngster would be made familiar with these various clusters of occupations and what is involved in entering them. In grades seven and eight he would concentrate on learning more about those particular job clusters that interest him most. In grades nine and ten he would select a job cluster to explore in some depth, an experience that would include visiting places where this kind of work is going on, trying his own hand at certain basic skills, and in general getting practical experience in what the line of work involves. In grades eleven and twelve he would pursue his selected job area even more intensely, in terms of three options: acquiring skills that would enable him to take a job immediately upon leaving high school; taking a combination of academic and on-the-job courses in preparation for entering a post-secondary institution that would train him as a technician, for instance; or electing a somewhat similar combination of courses in preparation for a professional degree from a four year college and beyond."

As to the second basic approach to career education discussed in the article from *American Education*, Marland explains the need to refocus education in terms of career interests.

In this section of the text we are looking at the Career Education cluster concept, which, while it may be a bit scary and overpowering in concept, is the heart of the Career Education program as enunciated by the U.S. Office of Education.

William F. Alexander promotes the premise that students may be trained in a core of skills common to many related occupations rather than focusing directly on a specific trade.

Walter W. Adams, Research and Development Specialist for the Center for Vocational and Technical Education, The Ohio State Univeristy, relates cluster development to Career Information Systems and to the HumRRO study from which a selection appears at the close of this section.

Patrick J. Weagraff discusses Career Education curriculum development using the cluster concept. He reviews the advantages and disadvantages of the use of clusters and concludes by supporting the concept.

L. Allen Phelps presents an analysis of cluster based instructional planning and relates it directly to industrial-arts Career Education.

The final selection in this section is an extract from a HumRRO study that explores the implications of cluster systems for the design of instruction.

William F. Alexander

CAREERS BY CLUSTER*

One of the gross misconceptions in secondary education is the idea students should be counseled into the general or college preparatory curriculum "just in case" the opportunity arises to go to college.

And, if it doesn't, there is always the vocational area which can prepare one for some type of job. Society as a whole seems to perpetuate this type of pedagogical class structure with small regard for the impact of the nation's growing technology.

U.S. Commissioner of Education Sidney Marland commented recently on this problem to the National Association of Secondary School Principals:

". . . A properly effective career education requires a new educational unity. It requires a breaking down of the barriers that divide our educational system into parochial enclaves.

"Our answer is that we must blend our curricula and our students into a single, strong secondary system. Let the academic preparation be balanced with the vocational or career program. Let one student take strength from another.

"And, for the future hope of education, let us end the divisive, snobbish, destructive distinctions in learning that do no service to the cause of knowledge, and do no honor to the name of American enterprise."

Dr. Marland adds "youngsters should be given the opportunity to explore eight, ten, a dozen occupations before choosing the one pursued in depth, consistent with the individual's ambitions, skills and interests."

Vocational programs for the '70s and '80s should be based on a broad cluster concept of skill development rather than those traditionally narrow trade programs operating in the public schools. The "Report on Manpower Requirements, Resources, Utilization, and Training" by the U.S. Department of Labor states:

"Whatever one concludes about the merits of broad versus occupationally oriented education, it is clear that more occupational curriculum offered at the high school and post-high school levels should be expanded. These curriculums should be based on the 'broad cluster' concept, as a part of broad based education, to permit both the opening of more options than are now available and the prospect of career ladders in these options."

---

*Dr. William F. Alexander–"Careers by Cluster" reprinted by permission from the December, 1972 issue of the NJEA REVIEW. Copyright © the New Jersey Education Association

Comments the U.S. Office of Education:

"Basic vocational education programs should be designed to provide education in skills and concepts common to clusters of closely related occupations. The curriculum should be derived from analyses of the common features of the occupations included.

"These students should receive specialized or more advanced vocational training later in post-high school programs, apprenticeship, or on-the-job experiences."

The career cluster concept holds that occupations may be classified into logically related groups on the basis of identical or similar elements. In vocational education and technical education, it provides for the organization of interrelated groups of industries or occupations into "families," "galaxies," or as the term implies "clusters," which have identical or similar problems, skills, and knowledges.

Several attempts to identify clusters have been made based on various criteria. For example, "clusters" may be derived from different dimensions, i.e., by similarities in job environment, hourly pay wage, educational requirement, psychomotor tasks, level of skill requirements (low skill, semi-skilled, high skill), and so on.

The dimension most commonly used is the similarity in trades or occupations. These "occupational clusters" have a high degree of overlapping tasks and related knowledge. Examples: health occupations, food service, accounting and bookkeeping, electricity and electronics, transportation, construction, personal services, and communications.

The U.S. Bureau of Adult, Vocational, and Technical Education has identified and codified 15 occupational clusters for use in career education (see accompanying artwork).

Basic premise is that students may be trained in a core of skills common to the number of related occupations rather than focusing directly on a specific trade. Furthermore, related information from science, physics, math, communications, and social studies is incorporated into the planning of clusters to provide a more useful and articulated program for students pursuing vocational programs.

Adapt Knowledge

Individuals trained under a vocational cluster concept have much more opportunity for occupational transfer and adaptation of knowledge, upward mobility within cluster areas, and a better understanding of the world of work and their role in it.

The cluster program is not conceived as a means for developing master craftsmen in any given trade. Rather, it provides opportunities for developing job entry-level skills and some second-level skills in related occupations.

The following chart shows interrelationships of clustered occupations, trade families, specific trades, and the artisan level of master craftsmanship. This pyramidal concept allows pupils to explore more fully the range of occupational potential and to develop at least entry-level skills in several occupations.

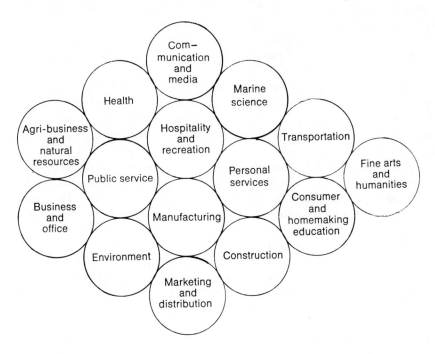

PYRAMIDAL CONCEPT OF CLUSTERED SKILLS*	
Artisan skills	Occupational refinement or retraining
Specific trades skills	Occupational specialization
Skills common to trade families	Occupational preparation
Skills common to clusters of occupations	Occupational exploration
Skills common to all occupations	Occupational awareness

*from "Project Career Quarterly Report," 1972

The cluster approach to career education is receiving a great deal of interest and attention in the past few years. A number of states are examining the potential of clusters in vocational education. Others—like New Jersey—are making efforts to establish career education programs which will, perhaps, utilize occupational clusters in some form. Very few, however, actually have pilot programs underway to develop and test cluster curriculum.

Several significant advantages in the cluster concept are summed up in the report of the U.S. Senate Committee on Labor and Public Welfare (commonly known as the Essex Report):

"1. To provide the student with greater flexibility in occupational choice patterns. This provides the student with an opportunity to obtain skills and knowledge for job entry in related occupations, and also an opportunity to appraise his own interest and abilities in relation to the several occupations in the cluster.

"2. To provide the student with vocational competence that affords him a greater degree of mobility is seen as being both geographic and on the job. The skills developed are seen as being both employable and transferable. The student who has the opportunity to prepare in a 'cluster' of occupations will likely be better prepared for technological change. Changes on the job will be expected rather than feared as in the past."

A number of industrial spokesmen have shown that workers will most likely change occupations two to seven times during their lifetime. This fact combined with the increasing geographical mobility of workers as well as industries calls for a different type of occupational training.

Develop General Skills

While there may be sacrifice in depth of skills compared to the present trade programs, there is a much broader-based understanding and general skill development in a family—or cluster—approach. It provides opportunity for a worker to move easily within the family of occupations allowing him to retain the element of choice and to avoid job obsoletion—ane probable termination.

Some writers have even urged adoption of cluster organization across the board in general education. (In this case, either subject area or occupational clusters may be used.)

Cluster development in vocational areas calls for a major change in conventional trade training programs which are criticized as being narrow in scope and inadequate in providing students with the flexibility and transferability of skills and knowledges necessary to keep pace with a changing technology.

For a student to spend two or even three years of time in a current secondary school trade program usually results in a great deal of time spent in in-depth skill development which is sometimes redundant and obsolete. In many instances, the trade program simply cannot keep pace with modern industrial machinery and practices and, therefore, improvises with whatever is available to the school.

Industry has found it quite satisfactory for employees to have a broad-based understanding and skill development in the industrial processes used and to allow the depth of technical skill to develop on the job.

   The reorganization of vocational training programs into occupational clusters may well provide a tenable solution we seek for educating for today—and for tomorrow.

Walter W. Adams

CAREER INFORMATION SYSTEM FOR THE COMPREHENSIVE CAREER EDUCATION SYSTEM*

Introduction

The 1960's may be marked as the most eventful decade in recent history. Historians will judge, but it should be safe to say that at least for us—the participants—it was a very eventful period. Of the many concerns that emerged during this time, one that relates to education is the explosion of knowledge. In 1963, Boston University hosted a conference in which several scholars presented papers on this theme. One scholar challenged the idea of the knowledge explosion by pointing out the widely accepted misconception that equates knowledge with information and, further, that equates the growth of knowledge with the shear accumulation of data. The presenter, Paul A. Weiss, stipulated that, "If one accepts this distinction, one readily perceives that this purported explosion is merely a glut of unassimulated data, rather than a spectacular breakthrough of deep insight and understanding." In his paper he defines knowledge as concepts, systems of thought and principles that through understanding, reduce the mass of data and experiences to their common denominators. I would like to employ the distinction made by Weiss, between information and knowledge, in our analysis of the educational uses of occupational information or, more specifically, to the task of defining and evaluating the advantages and disadvantages associated with alternative methods of organizing information about work for educational purposes.

Background and Rationale

The practice of grouping occupations is so common and pervasive that the existence of these schemes is hardly noticeable. In this regard, consider such

*Walter W. Adams—"Career Information System for the Comprehensive Career Education System" reprinted from *Career Education: Implications for Increased Educational Relevancy*, Robert E. Taylor (Ed.)

93

areas as industry, government, the military, civil service, or fields of work like medicine—each has its own occupational hierarchies and grouping schemes used to define status, responsibility, authority, promotion, or salary. Within education, occupations are frequently organized or grouped in some way for instruction in vocational education or in specific subject areas and for guidance, counseling, and placement purposes.

Now, with the advent of career education, the importance of organizing occupationa information has reached the unprecedented level for use within the total curriculum—there to be deliberately woven into the entire range of educational experiences. The new requirements associated with broad curriculum usage reveal the limitations and inappropriateness of most existing grouping systems. This places the responsibility for devising a new and more appropriate occupational clustering system squarely on our shoulders, as career educators.

The need for developing a comprehensive career clustering system for career education was recognized early by the United States Office of Education, in efforts described by Commissioner of Education Sidney Marland. Gordon Swanson identifies occupational clustering as an essential element of a career education program. Swanson stresses the importance of adopting an "orderly system for comprehending the enormous number of occupations which may be examined in the process of accepting, rejecting, or otherwise considering an occupational choice."

The occupational world consists of more than 21,000 defined occupations, with many of the same occupations having variations and differing emphasis that result in endless uniqueness. The massiveness and complexity of this type of information must be reduced through grouping, clustering, or some orderly organization to render it educationally manageable and useful. In its final form, the information must be organized so it is representative of work as it occurs both in the community and society. It must also be developed so it will be appropriate to the developmental level of students at various grade levels.

The initial steps in the development of the Comprehensive Career Education Model (CCEM) clustering system consisted of contracting with the Human Resources Research Organization (HumRRO) to locate or design an occupational clustering system suitable for career education. Our contract with HumRRO specified three general criteria. They were that the clustering system: (1) must encompass most existing jobs, (2) must be translatable into the design of an entire K-12 curriculum, and (3) must show clear and specific advantages over other clustering systems. HumRRO's final report provided us with two essential inputs, first a review and analysis of existing clustering systems and, second, a proposed model of a new clustering system for career education. This information enabled us to assess the state-of-the-art and provided us with a starting point to launch our own efforts in developing an occupational clustering system.

Three additional criteria were developed after analysis of the HumRRO report. These served to guide our efforts in determining what the final clustering system would be like. The new criteria were that the system: (1) must interface with existing occupational information resources, (2) must be accessible by different users for a variety of educational purposes, and (3) must possess a substantive structure and a uniform language for K-12 curriculum design purposes.

The first criterion to interface with existing occupational information resources was based upon the realization that it would not be feasible to redesign the world of work in view of the extensive requirements for information about it. Our goal is to bridge the gap between the school and work, which consists of maximizing interface with knowledge about work in our culture.

The second requirement is that occupational information be accessible by a variety of users, such as teachers, curriculum developers, and counselors, as well as students for instruction, guidance, counseling, career exploration, career preparation, and placement purposes. This criterion is based on recognition of the need to infuse a uniform and consistent interpretation of career information into all aspects of the educational program in a planned and articulated way. This is regarded as imperative to achieving continuous student growth in educational and career competency.

The third and most crucial of the new criteria relates to the curriculum concept of structure and is considered in two steps. The first consists of defining the content and parameters of the information required. The second involves determining how the information is to be structured in terms of the basic elements of work and their interrelationships.

Career Information

In light of the requirements of the CCEM for career information, it is obvious that we are no longer considering simple occupational information. Adopting the term "career information" becomes immediately more appropriate. This term is used by Isaacson to emphasize adding information about training and educational programs to information about jobs, thereby expanding the concept of occupational information to career information. In the CCEM, use of the term "career information" represents a further expansion of the concept to include, in addition to information about occupations and educational opportunities, labor market information on occupational demand, outlook, and economics and subject matter content knowledge. The expanded definition accents, either directly or indirectly, the following important concepts:

1. Career information is essential to the conduct of career education.
2. Career information is more encompassing than occupational information.
3. Programs of educational preparation are related to the development of occupational and career competency.
4. Subject matter content knowledge is related to performance of occupational tasks.
5. Educational and occupational experiences are enriched through career information.
6. Career development is facilitated by having information about changing community, state, and national labor market conditions.

7. Career development is facilitated by having information about changing educational and occupational requirements.
8. Career development is facilitated by having information about changing economic conditions.

Career information, defined in this way, establishes the foundation for attaining the goals of career education that relate to bridging the gap between the student and education, work, and society.

The CCEM definition of career information can be further delineated to express the interrelationships of its components—occupation, preparation, labor market, and content knowledge. The basic element of the definition is occupational information. What is new is recognition that the other elements of the definition help make occupational information relevant by enabling the student to relate his career plans and present educational experiences to anticipated educational and occupational opportunities. Information about occupations must be ordered in a fundamental way to provide a base for integrating the other forms of information specified in our definition. This is a probelm of structuring information about work and leads us to the next step in our discussion.

Career Information—Knowledge About Work

The problem of clustering career information is a problem of knowledge. The structure of knowledge in terms of "its connectedness and its derivations that make one idea follow another," according to Bruner, "is the proper emphasis in education" He further states that "the curriculum of a subject should be determined by the most fundamental understanding that can be achieved in the underlying principles that give structure to that subject." Determining structure, which consists of identifying the basic elements, concepts, or principles that give meaning to information about work, becomes the logical starting point.

Parenthetically, the entire career education curriculum and instructional program is also a matter of structure and design. The overall CCEM design is described elsewhere in Aaron J. Miller's paper entitled "The Emerging School-Based Comprehensive Career Education Model," and *Developmental Program Goals for the Comprehensive Career Education Model*, the latter available through the ERIC system. The total program design for career education is, in effect, a superstructure for organizing, coordinating, and integrating the program components. Successful integration of these components, one of which is career information, assures the prospect of developing an articulated K-12 career education program with sequenced and interrelated learning experiences.

Approaching organization of career information as a knowledge problem leads directly to the task of analyzing the knowledge base. The *Taxonomy of Educational Objectives, The Classification of Educational Goals, Handbook I: Cognitive Domain* provides a useful framework and helpful direction in this matter. Cognitive behavior is arranged within the taxonomy in terms of increasing complexity. As a hierarchical arrangement, "Knowledge" is considered to be the base or lowest level and is subdivided into three levels. The lowest level is "Knowledge of Specifics." This level describes, in terms of our concern, the overwhelming mass of specific job facts available. It is because information and data on occupations is proliferating at this level of knowledge, apart from an acceptable organizational scheme, that we are concerned about how to introduce career education into the curriculum. Resolution of the problem necessitates moving from the level of specific facts to a higher level of the taxonomy. There are essentially two higher levels of knowledge within the taxonomy that suggest how this may be achieved.

The first or next highest level that applies is entitled "Knowledge of Ways and Means of Dealing with Specific." It describes knowledge organized into classes or categories. This level is probably most descriptive of present efforts to organize or cluster information about occupations. Typical modes of organizing information about occupations. Typical modes of organizing information include classes, sets, divisions, categories, arrangements, and clusters developed for a given subject, purpose, or problem. An important factor to recognize is that the reasons for organizing information at this level vary and are frequently specific and narrow. The categories or classifications developed tend to serve the interests of those in a specific area or discipline and are difficult, if not impossible, to apply in other areas or to expand for wider use. In the area of our concern, schemes for organizing occupational information are typically geared to themes such as vocational interest, occupational information filing plans, subject matter, staffing arrangements, or funding plans.

Analysis of existing occupational clustering and grouping arrangements did not reveal any clustering scheme that met the information requirements of the CCEM. Our alternative was to develop a new clustering arrangement that could have been designed to meet specific curriculum requirements for occupational information, or could have been designed basically enough to meet the information requirements of all components within the career education program, as well as providing a base for interface with the community in terms of employers and relationships with other institutions. The second of these options is discussed next.

The highest level of knowledge in the taxonomy is "Knowledge of the Universals and Abstractions in a Field." This includes knowledge of theories and structures in the sense of identifying "the body of principles and generalizations along with their interrelations to present a clear systematic view of a complex phenomena, problem, or field." Organization of career information at this level correlates with our concern for structure and establishing a comprehensive knowledge base for a career information system.

The implications of this analysis are that the requirements for career information, created by the growing importance of career education, taken together with the increasing inundation of specific facts and bits of information about occupation, must be resolved by either adopting or developing a special purpose clustering system or by attempting to identify the basic structure for information about work. Both alternatives serve to order and arrange career information and reduce and eliminate overlap and redundancy. The positive educational features that occur in selecting the alternative to structure knowledge about work are succinctly stated by Beckner and Dumas:

Viewed as strictly as possible from the position of a theory of learning, Bruner's structural emphasis may be summarized in the following three propositions:

1. Learning occurs when isolated elements of 'knowledge' are so organized, connected, or arranged as to allow them to take on meaning for the learner.
2. Further learning is facilitated by the perception of an organized, meaningful pattern into which new experiences may be integrated easily and quickly.
3. Self-discovery of the unifying or structural elements, the 'organizing ideas,' of any body of knowledge and the organization or reorganization of these into larger patterns in order to discover larger meanings, serves as a powerful reward to the learner, reinforcing the present learning and motivating future efforts.

The Structure of Career Information Model

The Career Information Model (CIM) represents our efforts to develop an occupational clustering system. The CIM is a composite of several clustering and occupational information systems that have either been adopted or modified to achieve a single integrated model. The multidimensional nature of the CIM permits maximum interface with many other clustering approaches that are based upon similar concepts or that address the whole world of work. The CIM achieves maximum interface with existing sources of information about occupations, such as the *Occupational Outlook Handbook*, the Dictionary of Occupational Titles, and local, state, and national labor market information. In addition, the CIM provides for a logical flow of concepts about work expressed in elementary terms for the lower grades to more complex and detailed concepts about work at the upper grade levels. The model provides potential for maximum use of career information by all the participants in the education process. The substantive structure of the system helps to insure proper sequence and articulation of curriculum unit content and guidance in terms of language and concepts about work. It also serves as a base for integrating efforts of the various components of the career education program and coordinating community contacts as they relate to work.

The foundation for the CIM is the occupational definitions in Volume I of the DOT, *Definition of Titles*. The DOT represents the single most comprehensive and systematic organization of occupational information available within our culture. It is the legitimate base for a comprehensive career information system if knowledge about the entire scope of work found within our society is appropriate content for career education. The structure for organizing the base information for the CIM is derived from an analysis of Volume II of the DOT, *Occupational Classification.*

The knowledge structure consists of the most fundamental statement of underlying principles that can be derived. This is analogous to classifying matter as basically animal, mineral, or vegetable in the popular guessing game. Similarly, the concept "work" is considered to be reduceable to a structure of Product, Process, and the Person of the worker. Product includes *what* is done in terms of industry. Process refers to *how* work is done through tasks performed, and Person describes *who* does the work. The latter includes the significant characteristics and traits of the worker, including such factors as interest, aptitude, and educational development.

The occupational definitions in Volume I of the DOT serve as the information base and can be ordered or arranged in terms of each of the dimensions of the structure. This is possible because each definition includes information on the industry, tasks, and characteristics of the worker. The information base itself possesses the characteristic of being a cultural-linguistic (alphabetical) classification system, which means, of course, that if you can name it you can find it.

With the structure, one can start with a specific occupational title, find the definition, and follow it through the system to determine the relationship the occupation has to industry, tasks performed, and worker traits. Alternately, one can start with information related to any one dimension of the structure and trace it back to the information base or to either of the other two dimensions.

The utility of the CIM is exemplified in its adaptability. To illustrate: the Process or occupation dimension of the CIM includes information about tasks performed; as the tasks are identified, the skills and understandings required can easily be retified, the skills and understandings required can easily be related to an external organization of information about educational preparation and training programs. Thus, the CIM serves as an important link between information about work and education. The principle of linkage holds for many other types of external information as well. Among them are labor market demand, outlook, and economics, a variety of human work characteristics, and placement and follow-up information.

The CIM is therefore more than an occupational clustering system in the usual or popular sense; it is a structure of knowledge about work that serves to integrate a number of approaches to clustering, a multiple clustering system. As such, the CIM possesses the characteristics Piaget attributes to developmental structures. Piaget's characteristics of structure include: *wholeness* (in the sense of embracing all relevant information), *transformation* (in being able to relate and reorder information about work meaningfully), and *self-regulation* (in the sense of the structure having stability and direction for development).

The structure of knowledge about work is defined in the preceding manner. The initial criteria stipulated in the HumRRO contract, as well as the new requirements that emerged from our analysis of their report, are met in the CIM. In addition, by accepting the alternative to determine the structure of knowledge about work instead of devising a special-purpose clustering system the CIM

addresses squarely the mass of information available and the information requirements of CCEM. The CIM provides us with both a reasonable base from
which to develop career education programs and a framework to conduct required research activities.

Components—The Career Information Model

Basic model

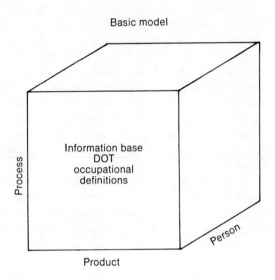

Definitions of Model Components

The Career Information Base—The information base for the CIM consists of the
21,741 occupations defined in Volume I of the DOT. The occupational definitions constituting the base possess two essential properties. The first is that each
definition is concise and includes: the occupational title, alternate titles, DOT
code number, industry identification, description of tasks performec, and indication of the worker characteristics. The second property is that the information in the occupational definitions can be organized into each of the three
perspectives of the CIM structure: Product—Industry, Process—Occupation, and
Person—Worker Traits.

1. *Product Information – Industry*—This perspective consists of grouping occupations in terms of the basic product or service provided. The groups are
   called industries or clusters. Specific occupations are arrayed vertically within the CIM cluster in terms of the variety of occupations related to creating
   the product or service. The following diagram illustrates the CCEM industry
   or cluster breakdown for each set of grade levels.

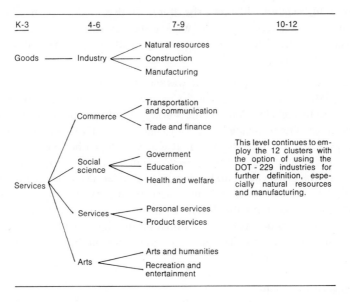

2. *Process Information—Occupations*—This perspective involves organizing the occupations arrayed vertically by cluster or industry into groups organized horizontally across the model. The resulting matrix serves to identify specific occupations with their related occupational groups. The grade level organization of the horizontal occupational groups is as follows:

Grades K—3—Occupations in the Goods and Services clusters can be grouped horizontally by the basic tasks performed. Managers, leaders, and policy-makers can be grouped together while technicians and craftsmen or general workers and employees can be organized into separate groups based on the common or related tasks performed by the workers.

Grades 4—6—The Five CCEM Clusters used at grades 4—6 are divided horizontally within the CIM into the nine Occupational Categories (first digit of DOT code number) of the DOT Occupational Group Arrangement (OGA).

Grades 7—9—The Twelve CCEM Clusters are divided into the eighty-three Occupational Divisions (first two digits of the DOT code number) of the DOT OGA.

Grades 10—12—The Twleve CCEM Clusters may continue to be used or expanded to the 229 Industries in the DOT. In either case, the eighty-three OGA Occupational Divisions may continue to be used or, in areas where greater specificity is required, such as guidance, placement, or career preparation, the OGA Occupational Groups (first three digits of the DOT code number) can be used. The potential in using Occupational Groups is to be able to divide the vertical industries into a maximum of the 603 occupational groups or levels.

3. *Person Information–Worker*–The third, or depth, dimension of the CIM relates to characteristics of the worker such as traits, aptitudes, and vocational interests. The grade level arrangement of information on worker characteristics is as follows:

Grades K–3–Information about worker characteristics relates to the question, "What is the worker like?" Consideration of this question at grades K–3 would include a look at the worker in terms of personal, physical, or educational factors related to performance of the basic occupational tasks.
Grades 4–6–The third dimension at grades 4–6 can be considered in terms of understanding the different levels of job functioning. The last of three digits of the DOT code number indicate the relationship an occupation has to different levels of significant functions with Data, People, and Things (DPT). Learning about the different functions involved in work permits the student to assess occupational information in relation to his preferences for selected job functions. The levels of job functions are as follows: (U.S. Department of Labor):

Hierarchies of Functions

	Data (4th digit)	People (5th digit)	Things (6th digit)
Highest	0 Synthesizing 1 Coordinating 2 Analyzing 3 Compiling 4 Computing 5 Copying 6 Comparing	0 Monitoring 1 Negotiating 2 Instructing 3 Supervising 4 Diverting 5 Persuading 6 Speaking-Signaling	0 Setting-up 1 Precision working 2 Operating-Controlling 3 Driving-Operating 4 Manipulating 5 Tending 6 Feeding-Offbearing

Lowest	7 No significant
	8 relationship
		7 Serving
		8 No significant
		  relationship
			7 Handling
			8 No significant
			  relationship

Grades 7–9–The Person dimension of the CIM can be approached at the career exploration level most effectively through the DOT Worker Trait Groups (WTG). This is an organization of occupational titles and definitions by worker traits. The WTGs represent occupations that are grouped together because of the similarity of their relationships to DPT and common trait requirements found in the WTG Qualifications Profile (QP). The QP is composed of estimates and/or actual measures of the trait requirements (Crites, 1969). The requirements are expressed in terms of the level of the trait necessary for satisfactory or average performance of the major occupational tasks (U.S. Department of Labor). The QP includes estimates or measures of General Educational Development (GED), Specific Vocational Preparation (SVP), aptitude, interest, temperament, and physical demands. The most useful information will probably include DPT, interest, and aptitude because this permits the student to assess the WTGs. The descriptions in the WTG include Work Performed, Worker Requirements, Clues for Relating Appli-

cants and Requirements, and Training and Methods of Entry. In addition, specific occupational titles are found on the pages following each WTG description.

Grades 10–12–At the career preparation level, information of a more definitive nature is available within the Worker Trait Arrangement (WTA). As the student becomes more proficient in stating and describing what he has learned about himself in more precise terms, he can use this information in evaluating and determining career preparation options.

The following diagram illustrates the CIM at grades 4–6 and shows how the dimensions of the model relate to each other in terms of the basic structure. The components of the CIM as illustrated in the diagram show how the dimensions of the model relate to each other. Graphic examples can also be developed for the other grade level ranges (K–3, 7–9, and 10–12). An important consideration is not whether the dimensions of the CIM are orthogonally related as depicted in the cubistic model, but whether the dimensions consittute a valid structure of knowledge about work. If so, we are provided with a means of organizing career information and giving it substantive meaning. The next step is to describe the relationships of the CIM to the overall CCEM design and to indicate how the system can be operationalized in the form of the Career Information System (CIS).

CCEM Career Information Model: Grades 4–6

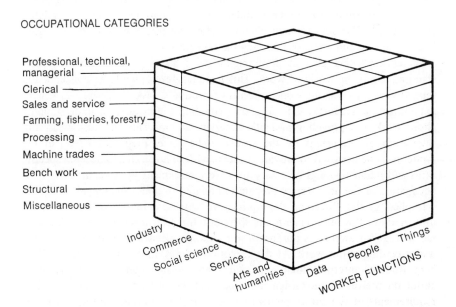

OCCUPATIONAL CATEGORIES

Professional, technical, managerial
Clerical
Sales and service
Farming, fisheries, forestry
Processing
Machine trades
Bench work
Structural
Miscellaneous

Industry
Commerce
Social science
Service
Arts and humanities
Data
People
Things
WORKER FUNCTIONS

The Career Information System

The CCEM design identifies major emphases within the overall career education program. The major thrust of the program changes for selected grade ranges in the model, giving direction for program development and delivery of career education through curriculum and guidance. The following diagram shows the major developmental emphases of the CCEM design.

Career Development Emphasis in the CCEM

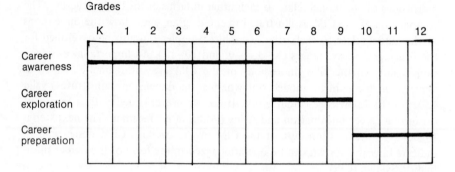

At grades K–6 program focus is on development of career awareness. The primary emphasis at grades 7–9 is career exploration, while at grades 10–12 attention is given to career preparation. At each of these levels the overriding objective of the program is to provide students with educational experiences related to the design. The question now becomes, How can career information be organized to support and improve achieving the objectives of the design?

Career awareness aims at development of a broad base of general understanding about the world of work. This includes developing basic concepts and related vocabulary about work in terms of products, tasks, and workers. Career exploration at grades 7–9 focuses on extending the breadth of understanding about work and providing in-depth experiences, especially in those areas considered to be important by the student. The career preparation level of the model is to be designed to provide students with opportunity to develop specific skills and understandings necessary for career placement in either an entry-level occupation or the next step of preparation related to their career goals.

Implied in the foregoing description are extensive requirements for career information. The requirements are different for each level of the model. This means that for awareness purposes information is needed to help develop broad understanding about work. At the exploration level, information is required to help students interpret their experiences and relate emerging understandings about themselves to knowledge about occupations or broad areas of work. The requirements at the career preparation level include having information about specific occupations, preparation requirements, related instructional modules, courses and preparation programs, post-secondary educational programs, and placement opportunities.

The dimensions of the CIM relate to the CCEM design and information requirements. In the discussion of the CIM, each dimension of the model was shown to have a level of information appropriate for each of the grade ranges. Now we are interested in relating a basic aspect of the structure of work and its corresponding dimension in the CIM to each of the levels of the CCEM design. This involves the determining dimension of the CIM that relates to the major emphasis of the CCEM design and utilizing it as the basic framework for organizing career information for that level of the model. The fact that the dimensions of the CIM are coordinated and interrelated help to guarantee a balanced approach to career education at all levels. In this regard, all of the dimensions of the CIM are useful at each level of the CCEM design, even though one is selected as the primary mode of organizing career information. The following diagram illustrates the relationship of the CIM and the CCEM design.

Interface: CCEM Design and CIM

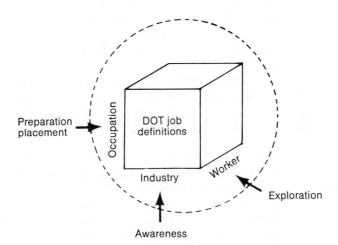

The following discussion relates to possible modes of organizing career information in relation to the CCEM design. The suggestions made here pertain to developing the actual content of the Career Information System (CIS). At the present time, content for the lower grade levels is in the process of being developed. At the higher grade levels the content will in all likelihood be developed or consist of appropriate commercial materials in both hard copy and data base form for computerized use. These components of the CIS (grades 7–9 and 10–12) will not be developed until further conceptualization is completed for these levels of the CCEM. Discussion of the CIS for our present purpose is limited to the organization of the K-3 and 4–6 levels.

The focus of career education at grades K–6 is career awareness. The unique information requirements at this level are associated with developing breadth of understanding about the work, through an organized curricular approach. This requirement can be met through an organization of career information by the Industry dimension of the CIM. The CIS for grades K–3 and 4–6 is described as follows:

1. At grades K–3, the content of the CIS is organized by Industry–Goods and Services. It consists of occupational briefs (11" x 14" cards) filed alphabetically within two clusters. Each card is labeled with the occupation and cluster titles. The front of the card has a drawing of the worker performing a basic job task(s) with a simple definition of the occupation. The reverse side of the card consists of three sets of statements in large print, with key vocabulary words underlined. The statements are grouped by Industry, Tasks Performed, and Worker Characteristics. It is expected that the CIS will have approximately 130 to 190 representative occupations in the K-3 kit.
2. At grades 4–6, the CIS is organized by the Five CCEM clusters. The content of the CIS will consist of single page briefs developed for each occupation. The briefs are expected to be color-coded by cluster and organized within each cluster by DOT code number (first digit). Each brief will have the occupational title, cluster identification, and a sketch of the worker performing a major occupational task(s). The basic occupational information related to the CIM structure is contained in descriptions of the related Industry, Tasks Performed, and Worker Characteristics. In addition, related subject matter content, general preparation requirements, and basic economics about the occupation will be included. It is anticipated that the grades 4–6 CIS will contain approximately 400 occupations.

Efforts to identify and develop content for the CIS have been carefully coordinated with the CCEM curriculum development process. The occupation content for both K–3 and 4–6 CIS was selected by meeting one of the following criteria: (1) an occupation and related information had to be required by a curriculum unit; (2) the occupation, if not directly covered in a curriculum unit, had to be representative of an area or level of work, as determined by the CIM; or (3) an occupation, if it is indigenous to a particular community or geographical region (such as an occupation in automobile manufacturing), had to be representative of a major visible area of work. A final consideration in regard to content is to make provision for teachers and local curriculum developers to add new content to help them localize the CIS content and add support for infusing career education into other curriculum units and class activities.

This is our progress to date. Opportunities for research and development in this area are numerous and promising. The potential contribution to American education is great, especially the emerging form—career education. Knowledge about work organized in a basic integrative way is regarded as an important aspect of the total CCEM. The proper blend of knowledge about work, with the body of content knowledge already the "stock and trade" of education, and knowledge of human growth and development are our most basic resources. The task is to transform them into validated educational programs. The first step of the transformation process is conceptualization—that is where we are. The next step is to operationalize the program through research and development—that is where we hope to go.

Summary

In the course of this discussion, the task of clustering occupations or occupational information for educational purposes has been considered from the point of view of the CCEM. Initially, attention was called to the larger issue of whether to define occupational clustering as essentially a problem of information or knowledge. The implications of defining occupational clustering as a problem of knowledge led to consideration of special classification schemes and structuring as alternatives. In this examination, preference was given to structuring knowledge about work as the most practicable way of meeting the information requirements of a comprehensive career education program. The concept of occupational information was expanded to career information and the Career Information Model developed to correlate with the structure of knowledge about work. The developmental features of the CCEM design were considered as they relate to the CIM, and the resulting interface provided direction for development of the Career Information System. Aspects of the CIS are now in development, and implications for its continued development are inherent in the structure of knowledge about work and the CIM. We hope we are approaching the point where efforts can be initiated to validate these concepts through research.

Patrick J. Weagraff

CAREER EDUCATION CURRICULUM DEVELOPMENT USING THE CLUSTER CONCEPT*

It is indeed paradoxical that in a country which has traditionally placed high value on the world of work and the ethic, we face the reality that for many the curriculum in our schools largely prepared them only for the next higher level on the educational ladder.

If you believe as some of us do that this paradox represents a clue to one of the real problems of our contemporary curriculum, then you should be interested in what the cluster framework in career education is and how it is bringing about drastic changes in curriculum patterns and organization.

Career Education Organization

It is difficult to say where or when career education began since it is not a well defined program. At best, it can be described as an evolving but durable concept. Under different labels, it has emerged repeatedly and with increasing frequency on the American scene.

Career education is best described as a systematic way to acquaint students with the world of work in their elementary and junior high school years, as well as to prepare them in high school and college to enter and advance in a career field chosen from among many.

Most practitioners divide career education into four interrelated phases. Phase I, which is concerned with developing student awareness, occurs in the elementary school during grades 1–6. This awareness phase explores questions as: What are occupations? Who works in these occupations? How do the workers accomplish their jobs? Phase II is a prevocational and exploratory experience occurring in grades 7, 8, and 9. It involves classroom instruction, experiences and observation. Phase III begins in about grade 10 and allows each student to

*Patrick J. Weagraff–"Career Education Curriculum Development Using the Cluster Concept" reprinted from the Summer, 1973 issue of *Educational Horizons* by permission of Pi Lambda Theta.

explore more deeply a single occupational cluster or begin specialized training. Phase IV takes place in the last years of high school or in a post-secondary institution.

The intent of this article is not to reiterate the philosophical rationale or even the imperative need for a comprehensive career education system. This is being well documented by prominent scholars throughout our nation, many of whom have articles appearing in this publication. It is the intent, however, to provide a simple overview of the cluster system and the implications resulting from its use as a means of organizing career education curriculum.

Cluster Framework

The problems of delivering a comprehensive career education are compounded by the complexity of the American economy and diversity of the American labor force. The *Dictionary of Occupational Titles*, and the Department of Labor catalog, for example, lists more than 45,000 jobs which exist today. Obviously, dealing with each of these individual jobs would be administratively impossible when designing and implementing a career awareness program or when providing other aspects of career education. The only feasible solution seems to be to group these jobs into a series of manageable clusters. While it is not possible to deal with twenty thousand separate jobs, it would be feasible to deal with 15 or 20 broad career clusters.

Any scheme which is developed for clustering jobs for career education purposes should meet four basic requirements:

1. The cluster scheme should be such that it encompasses all or most of the jobs in the *Dictionary of Occupational Titles*. In other words, after the cluster scheme has been established, it should be possible to fit most jobs in the *Dictionary of Occupational Titles* into some one of the career clusters which have been designated.
2. Each cluster should include jobs at all levels, from entry-level through skilled jobs, technical jobs, and professional jobs. That is to say, each cluster should contain a logical career ladder of jobs requiring increasing levels of education.
3. Each cluster should be related to an identifiable group of employers. For example, if we have a cluster in the health occupations, it is possible to identify within the community a group of potential employers, such as hospital administrators, private physicians, and dentists, who could relate to this particular cluster. Similarly, if we have a cluster in the construction occupations it is possible to identify in a given community various construction contractors and construction firms who could relate to this career cluster.
4. The clusters should be enduring over time. That is, each cluster should represent a continuing societal function which will be carried on throughout

the foreseeable future. For example, it can be assumed that for the forseeable future our society will be manufacturing things, constructing things, transporting things and providing health services for the people. Therefore, clusters in the manufacturing occupations, the construction occupations, the transportation occupations, and the health occupations are likely to be enduring over time. Although individual jobs within these clusters may be phased out due to technological change, other new and emerging jobs will appear in each cluster to take the place of those phased out. If an individual has had well-rounded training in the common core of a particular cluster, his flexibility for moving to another job within that cluster will be facilitated, should his present job disappear as a result of technological change. Having mastered the common core of the cluster, he would be able, with a minimum amount of retraining, to move to another type of emerging job within that same cluster. This will provide individuals with the flexibility needed to cope with the changing nature of our economy and our labor force.

The U.S. Office of Education has developed a cluster scheme which, it is believed, meets the four requirements specified above. This cluster scheme consists of 15 career clusters, which are:

Business and Office Occupations
Marketing and Distribution Occupations
Communications and Media Occupations
Construction Occupations
Manufacturing Occupations
Transportation Occupations
Agri-Business and Natural Resource Occupations
Marine Science Occupations
Environmental Control Occupations
Public Service Occupations
Health Occupations
Hospitality and Recreation Occupations
Personal Service Occupations
Fine Arts and Humanities Occupations
Consumer and Homemaking Occupations

All types of jobs are included in these fifteen clusters, from basic entry level positions to those which require advanced degrees.

The term cluster has taken on a variety of meanings. It may refer to a single grouping of seemingly like jobs, to institutional groups such as transportation, manufacturing or public service. Within the context of career education, it has come to be associated with a broad framework around which instruction at differing age levels can be structured.

The cluster framework, as it has emerged in career education, provides an individual with an early awareness of careers. Children in the early grades deal with the major concepts of the cluster. For example, "moving things and people from here to there" is the major concept students should be aware of when studying the transportation cluster. As students progress, they have exploratory learning opportunities culminating in hte development of job entry competencies.

Many teachers and schools use the cluster framework as a means to orient students to careers. At the elementary·level, all clusters are studied. In grades 7 and 8, a student may choose to study five or six clusters. By grades 9 or 10, this exploration process may narrow down to one or more areas. In grades 11 and 12, students may concentrate their career preparation in one cluster.

The theory behind the cluster framework is that 97 percent of the approximately 45,000 occupational titles can be grouped into a few cluster areas according to similar characteristics and purposes. Usually the cluster is broken down into its major occupational groups and then into its various jobs. For example, the construction cluster has several occupational groups including: masonry, wood, electrical, plumbing, pipefitting, and sheet metal. Within these, occupations would include: carpenter, tile-setter, surveyor, roofer, cement finisher, and electrician, to name but a few of the several hundred jobs in construction.

Instructional methods using the occupational cluster framework might include on-site observations, hands on laboratory experience, role-playing, and many other appropriate activities.

Implications of the Cluster Framework

With the increased use of cluster frameworks, many implications seem to be evident. Among these are the following:

1. Career education in general, and more specifically the cluster approach, will bring about massive changes in instructional prodùcts. Few instructional materials are available for career education, particularly at the elementary level. New career oriented products and "learning systems" are being developed by several large publishers and media organizations. While these products are starting to appear on the market, it won't be until late 1974 that they are generally available.
2. Cooperative or work experience education is becoming a more common pattern of curriculum organization. Most work experience programs in the past have been vocational in nature. The use of a cluster framework is resulting in work experience programs which are largely exploratory or pre-vocational in their intent.
3. If the cluster framework is widely adopted, a greatly expanded vocational education program at the secondary level will result. Traditionally, vocational education has dealt with only a few occupational areas such as agriculture or trade and industrial occupations. Programs in new career clusters such as public service, marine science, and communications will start to emerge in secondary schools.

4. The experience of school districts who have implemented the cluster approach indicate it is much easier to infuse the clusters into the curriculum of the self-contained classroom taught by a generalist than into a subject-centered program taught by a specialist. Since most elementary schools are self-contained, it follows that the greatest immediate impact of the cluster approach will be at the elementary level.
5. The cluster framework will call for more integration of the disciplinary subject matter in the high school. With the explosion of subjects competing for a place in the curriculum, it seems reasonable that English, science, mathematics, and social studies have some degree of relevancy to one or more clusters.
6. Since use of a cluster approach required optimum use of outside resources, we could easily shift to a community school curriculum pattern.
7. There is some evidence to indicate that the cluster framework blends exceptionally well with team teaching and use of instructional units at the classroom level. Accordingly, both team teaching and unit organization are taking on increased emphasis in schools where career education is being implemented.

Limitations of Cluster Approach

While the cluster framework has a promising future, there are many limitations that must be recognized and dealt with:

1. The cost of implementing a comprehensive cluster system really is not known at this time. Full implementation of a cluster system in K–12 situations could cost 5 to 8 times the amount of current state and federal appropriations.
2. The clusters have a large amount of "overlap." For example, are jobs in the parks field a part of public service, natural resources, or recreation, hospitality and tourism? Failure to adequately define the clusters could result in costly duplication of instruction.
3. No single set of clusters exist. There are groups of clusters which tend to describe what a worker does. Still other cluster systems are rooted in the sociological or psychological complexities of occupational choice and worker function.
4. A cluster framework must have a balanced program to be successful. Programs dealing with career orientation need to be followed by skill programs for those careers. This usually means that a school district has to enlarge its vocational and adult education components. In this period of educational belt tightening, this may be more a dream than reality.
5. Our educational system is not in a position to absorb large numbers of students in any comprehensive cluster system. Many schools are too small, others have specialized or separate vocational facilities. Thus, the capacity of our educational system to respond to a cluster framework is limited.

Summary

The advantages and the disadvantages of a cluster system are formidable. We know the installation and operation of a cluster approach to career education is meaningful, realistic, costly, and viable. We also know it can only be implemented after considerable diligence and hard work on the part of administrators and teachers working as a team with their students, parents, and community.

It has been said that neophobia—the fear of anything new—will plague development of career education and the cluster approach. While this is undoubtedly true, we must accept the fact change is required if we are to effectively implement career education. Hopefully, neophobia will not stop you from exploring the use of cluster approach in your career education program.

L. Allen Phelps

CLUSTER BASED INSTRUCTIONAL PLANNING FOR INDUSTRIAL-ARTS CAREER EDUCATION*

What is career education? What is the role of industrial education relative to career education? How can I, as an industrial-arts teacher, become an integral part of the career education of my students?

These basic questions which many industrial-arts teachers are asking today— and their answers—might provide insight into the possibility and probability of industrial-arts teachers fulfilling a leadership role in the development and implication of career education.

The emerging concept of career education has many definitions and descriptors. The ultimate purpose of career education, however, appears to be the preparation of people of all ages, and all levels of educational attainment, for successful careers in the world of work.

Further expansion of this basic definition will identify several inclusive concepts. These include: career awareness, career exploration, career development, home and family education, multifaceted community involvement, diversified learning environments, interdisciplinary subject matter correlation, and "hands-on" learning experiences.

The emerging vehicle for coordinating these components in an instructional program appears to be the industry/occupational cluster. The cluster concept, which will be outlined in greater detail later, will provide a realistic basis for implementing the career education program.

Five Goals for IA

As a discipline, industrial-arts education appears well down the road in attempting to achieve some of the goals of career education. The following five goals for

---

*L. Allen Phelps—"Cluster Based Instructional Planning for Industrial Arts Career Education," reprinted by permission from the April, 1973 issue of *School Shop*. Copyright 1973 by Prakken Publications, Inc.

industrial arts, which were presented in *A Guide to Improving Instruction in Industrial Arts*, appear to have a very definite career education orientation:

1. Develop insight and understanding of industry and its place in our culture.
2. Discover and develop talents, aptitudes, interests, and potentialities of individuals for technical pursuits and applied sciences.
3. Develop an understanding of industrial processes and the practical application of scientific principles.
4. Develop basic skills in the proper use of common industrial tools, machines, and processes.
5. Develop problem-solving and creative abilities involving the materials, processes, and products of industry.

Understanding the role of industry in our culture assists students in understanding the technological aspects of our society, and themselves as members of that society. Self-awareness and career awareness are basic components of career education.

The second goal of discovering and developing talents and aptitudes definitely implies both self-awareness and career exploration.

In determining the practical application of certain scientific principles students are again involved in assessing the "wholeness" of a technical society. Through this experience general education concepts, such as math and science, become meaningfully related to the world of work.

Basic skill development through "hands-on" experiences is an important part of career education. Basic skills in the use of tools, machines, and processes enable students to explore occupational clusters and the world of work even further.

Creativity and problem-solving skills are functional components of career selection, career preparation, and occupational advancement.

By actively implementing these discipline goals within the context of career education, industrial-arts educators should find themselves among the leaders of the career-education movement.

How to Get Involved

The remaining question to be discussed is: How can the industrial-arts teacher become actively involved in implementing career education?

As indicated earlier, the purpose and content of industrial arts is basically career-oriented, so major revisions are not required here. Major revisions do appear to be needed in the area of content presentation. Industrial-arts teachers need to restructure the presentation of their course content so it relates directly to occupational clusters which are representative of the world of work. This restructuring may be achieved by a variety of methods; however, a redesign of the instructional planning format appears to be the most effective.

CLUSTER: Communications and media	INSTRUCTIONAL CONCEPT:		Module Id./ Sequence Code CCM - 612
SUBCLUSTER: Drafting/Illustration	Construction of residential floor plans		

Behavioral learning outcomes:

Given specific tools, materials, equipment and requisite knowledge at his level of instruction, upon completion of the module the learner will be able to:

		IA Index
1. Analyze floor plan designs critically.		2, 3
2. Design an efficient floor plan from given room designations and minimum room dimensions.		1
3. Sketch a basic floor plan to approximate scale.		1, 2
4. Construct a complete and finished set of coordinated floor plans for a multi-level dwelling.		2
5. Prepare an accurate job description for the occupation of residential designer.		4

Suggested Instructional Activities	Modes of Instruction	Supportive Media
Teacher-led class discussion of floor plan design considerations	Teacher Group Peer	Transparencies
Students bring floor plan prints to class and discuss design	Professional	Floor plan print
Architect/Designer visits class to discuss floor plan designs and describe his occupations		
Class reviews floor plan design concepts by viewing "Residential Planning"	Para- professional	16mm film
Individual students needing reinforcement of specific floor plan design concepts views "Floor Plan" series	Self	8mm loop
Students design and prepare floor plan sketches and prints through individual lab experiences	Teacher Para- professional	

Figure 1   The Cluster Based Instructional Planning Module

More specifically, a cluster-based instructional planning module (Fig. 1) has been proposed and successfully tested as an effective instructional planning tool for career educators. This planning module contains several components. Each component reflects an essential element for the planning of career education instruction.

Cluster The USOE has identified 15 occupational clusters as the basis for implementing career education (Fig. 2). Industrial-arts content is identifiable in all 15 of the clusters, since they are industry based. At the present time, however, industrial-arts programs are only covering about 50 percent of these clusters. Industrial-arts program content is easily recognizable in the manufacturing, construction, transportation, and communications and media clusters.

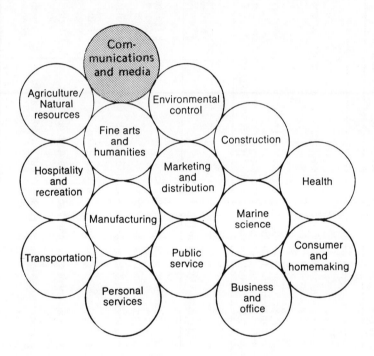

Figure 2 The 15 USOE Occupational Clusters

Subcluster Each cluster can be logically divided into subclusters. The subcluster will often represent course titles common to industrial arts and related disciplines. Some typical subclusters for the communications and media cluster are shown in Fig. 3.

Figure 3   Subclusters for the Communications and Media Subcluster

Instructional Concept   The instructional concept represents the title or topic of the planning module. Each subcluster can be divided into numerous instructional concepts. Following identification of the instructional concept, the module can be appropriately identified and/or sequenced in relation to the cluster and subcluster

Behavioral Learning Outcomes   These statements represent the terminal performance objectives for the module: an extensive, behavioral description of what the learner must be able to do in order to successfully complete the module. For the student, behaviorally stated outcomes focus on the information to be learned and eliminate guesswork. They are intended to be observable measures of student achievement.

IA Index   Each of the learning outcomes is numerically indexed to the goals for industrial-arts education which were stated earlier. This index/reference provides teachers with a checklist. Each module should include learning outcomes designed to satisfy *at least three* of the general goals of industrial arts. This index exists in order that industrial-arts teachers may maintain their discipline goals in relation to the goals of career education.

Suggested Instructional Activities A variety of different instructional activities is listed in this section. Different activities for achieving the behavioral outcomes are listed so the teacher may select the most appropriate activities for individual students. Usually there are several ways to teach a given concept, and each method or activity may be appropriate for a different type of learner.

Modes of Instruction The suggested instructional activities may conceivably be performed without the teacher. Certain instructional activities may be effectively administered by a paraprofessional, small group discussion, peer instruction, or self-instruction.

Supportive Media Audiovisual aids are a proven asset to most instructional activities. This section of the module lists certain audiovisual aids which may be necessary or helpful for specific instructional activities.

The cluster-based instructional planning module provides industrial-arts teachers with both a rationale and a vehicle for readily adopting a career education program. It essentially provides for: 1) relating small units of industrial-arts instruction (concepts) to occupational clusters primarily for the purpose of career exploration, 2) individualizing instruction activities to meet the needs of individual students, and 3) measuring student achievement and progress by behavioral outcomes rather than time dimensions.

John E. Taylor, Ernest K. Montague
and Eugene R. Michaels

IMPLICATIONS OF CLUSTER SYSTEMS FOR THE DESIGN OF INSTRUCTION*

This section will relate the use of clustering systems for the design of instruction of the entire K–12 sequence. Clustering systems can offer a major planning vehicle for preparing student-learning experiences, but they cannot be used as the sole input for the total curriculum. There are two important reasons for this qualification.

The first reason is that there lies at the base of all education the instruction in cognitive skills. They are the broad-base tool skills—reading, writing, and arithmetic—which are applicable in a myriad contexts. We use them to gather information, communicate with other people, and function in our daily lives. To equip students with these skills is to prepare them implicitly for future social and occupational roles.

The second reason arises from the structure of higher educational institutions. They serve as the major doorkeepers to many careers, especially those in the professions. The curriculum they stipulate for entry determines to a large extent the structure of high school offerings. The student without that academic preparation cannot have entry into higher education and therefore into our society's most remunerative and prestigious occupations.

These two inputs into the K–12 curriculum—instruction in cognitive skills and the relationship of higher educational institutions to career entry—obviously cannot be ignored in adapting K–12 curriculum for career education.

Clustering Systems as a Major Input into the Design of Instruction

The past use of clustering systems in an educational context has been confined to vocational education, usually to the last two years of high school training.

*John E. Taylor, Ernest K. Montague and Eugene R. Michaels—"Implications Of Cluster Systems For The Design Of Instruction" from *An Occupational Clustering System and Curriculum Implications for the Comprehensive Career Education Model,* January, 1972. Reprinted by permission of HumRRO Human Resources Research Organization.

121

The student receives, for the most part, training in specific job skills that will allow him entry into a series of specific jobs. A less common variation is to furnish the student with various broad skills that he can apply in several job contexts or situations.

We cannot expand this limited use of clustering systems by simply extending such use to the general K−12 instructional sequence. Too much is lacking for career development: The means by which students acquire information about careers are missing, as are the means by which a student can relate his personal goals, needs, and talents to possible career roles.

Because there have been few actual applications in schools, the conceptual base that might have arisen from past educational use of clustering systems cannot be borrowed to design an entire K−12 curriculum. We have combined clustering systems that were originally conceived for noneducational purposes in order to arrive at an inclusive system, usable in a general education context.

If a clustering system is to serve as a major input into instructional design, it must be useful in three ways:

To provide students with accurate and comprehensive information about what it means to work.

To provide a set of learning experiences against which a student can weigh his personal interests, needs, and talents in order to arrive at a candidate set of careers for his future adult roles.

To provide planning models that will help shape the general curriculum in terms of instructional objectives, content, and methods.

No clustering system is presently in operation that fulfills the three instructional functions—*information, guidance,* and *curriculum planning.* To design a system meeting these requirements meant that an unidimensional or single method of clustering had to be rejected. It would be too inflexible and confining. Only a set of multidimensional clusters would solve the problem imposed by the three functions.

The Dimensions of the Proposed Clustering System

The dimensions of the proposed clustering system, discussed at length in the previous sections, address the requirements of the three functions. The dimension of career levels stresses the need to provide learning experiences offering information to students about the impact of careers on personal life style and social status. The dimension of career areas stresses job content and function.

Learning experiences prepared along this dimension at first acquaint students with occupational roles and relate the skills and capabilities they acquire to occupational areas. As they advance toward career selection, more and more of their learning experiences are directed toward preparation in skills and knowledges needed for job entry. Thus, the instructional system must establish a basis for career selection through information and guidance and provide concrete skills and abilities for job entry through the curriculum.

The proposed clustering system in only one major source of the curriculum content. Because the outcomes of the CCEM are open-ended—the student can opt for job entry, college entry, post-secondary training, or any combination of these—the curriculum content is defined by the entry requirements of higher educational institutions, business, industry, and unions. The clustering system makes its largest input into the curriculum content by translating the skills and knowledges needed for job entry into learning experiences.

The essential role of the proposed clustering system is that of a planning vehicle. From it arises the means to plan learning experiences centered around career information and guidance. It also provides the means to derive the content necessary for job entry.

The Necessity of Coordinating the Clustering System
Within a Curriculum Structure

Since the clustering system serves chiefly as a planning guide, its inputs to the K—12 curriculum have to be placed within a curriculum structure that can accommodate them within the present organization of elementary and high schools.

Past attempts at translating job clusters into curriculum content have relied heavily upon general learning taxonomies, such as those proposed by Bloom, Gagne, and Fine. The purpose of these taxonomies is to cohere and sequence the learning experiences derived from a task analysis of job skills. Fine, for example, regards the categories of "Data, People, and Things" as a way to structure job skills for learning purposes. Any job task is to be placed within one of these categories, and it can be assigned to a hierarchy within the category, depending upon the degree of complexity of the skill. Under the "Data" category, a skill such as checking two sheets of numbers to see whether any mistakes were made in transcribing would be assigned to the lowest level—"Comparing." Bloom and Gagne have similar classificatory schemes prepared for cognitive skills and all learning, respectively, which can be applied to a task analysis of jobs.

These taxonomies have limited application to the present problem. First of all, a task-analytic approach to clustering jobs on the basis of common learning requirements has had only a few empirical examples in a severely limited set of occupations. The prior research that is a necessary antecedent to the broad educational use of these taxonomies has not been accomplished. Secondly, the use of these taxonomies has been confined to training in skills leading to immediate job entry, usually in programs of short duration. Job entry is only one of several outcomes of the CCEM. Awareness, Orientation, Exploration, and Selection are prior goals that the curriculum structure must address to realize career development. These taxonomies cannot provide a curriculum structure usable throughout the K—12 grades.

A series of constraints are imposed by the nature of the school-based model. Since the CCEM is to function within the present school system and its institutional arrangements without severe displacements, a curriculum structure must be devised that is in harmony with the present organization of school—certainly not one that is antagonistic to its institutional arrangements. These constraints alone would mitigate against the use of theoretical taxonomical structures. They have not been validated empirically, and to recommend the thorough and radical reorientation they would demand in terms of time, money, and additional physical resources would be to complicate a complex undertaking with unnecessary variables.

The curriculum structure that will be discussed in the next section is proposed as a means for adapting the present curriculum structure to career education with minimal displacements. It takes into account the goals and outcomes of the CCEM, the present institutional arrangements of schools, and the range of probable inputs influencing the content of the curriculum.

The Nine Processes Determining the Structure of Curriculum

It is proposed that the learning experiences that will equip students to meet one or several of the multiple outcomes can be contained within nine educational processes:

Communication
Social, Political and Economic
Art
Tool and Handcraft
Physical Development
Interpersonal
Mathematical
Scientific
Technological.

Groups of skills and capabilities that students need for career entry can be placed into the processes, once the students have chosen a set of careers or a specific career to follow. The processes can contain the content students need for college entry. Additionally, the processes can contain learning experiences that are coordinated with the progression that the CCEM has stipulated for career development: Awareness, Orientation, Exploration, and Selection. Most importantly, the proposed clustering system can work in conjunction with the processes to plan learning experiences that guide, inform, and equip students for the world of work.

The term "processes" has been chosen because it best conveys the nature and type of learning that should occur. We conceive of the learner as actively engaged in the processes of learning, where the importance of specific content acquisition is secondary to what the content enables the learner to do. Acquisition of scientific facts and concepts are not ends in themselves, but are tools that the learner can use to investigate and solve problems. Under this process approach, career development can be integrated with the instructional program. The student, in using the conceptual tools of science to solve problems, learns an important aspect of what scientists do as a function of their careers.

More than anything else, the process stresses an orientation rather than a pure category system for nine areas of learning. A pure category system is not possible for several reasons. Learning in certain areas, especially in the sciences and mathematics, has been organized into formal disciplines, and careers are built upon these disciplines. To be a physicist, chemist, or mathematician requires pursuit within the discipline and its organized body of methodology and knowledge. Acquiring cognitive skills that are generic in their application to many contexts constitutes another subdivision of learning processes. Finally, career specific processes—working with tools and machinery and applying various intellectual techniques in a work context—define another grouping of learning processes.

Because we cannot organize the content of the curriculum into homogeneous categories, the nine processes must reflect the differences among different kinds of content the student is to learn. However, the use of the term, process, underscores the need for arranging instructional objectives and methods that allow the student to be an active participant in the learning activity. With the perspective that the term implies, the career context falls in as a matter of course. The things a student learns to do have a real and functional context: what it presently enables him to do and what it will enable him to do in future social roles. Moreover, because of the career context, he continually sees the relationship of people working in various career areas to those skills and knowledges he presently is acquiring.

During grades K–6, the nine processes are combined into six main tracks. Communication and Social, Political and Economic processes are combined into one track. Mathematical, Scientific, and Economic processes are also grouped together into another track. The other four processes are on separate tracks. During grades 7–8, the only grouping is to combine Scientific and Technological processes. During grades 9–10 each process forms its own track.

Each process is seen as containing much of the content that presently is taught in elementary and high schools. Three of them were added to include content from career areas not generally present in elementary schools and the first two years of high school. These are Tool and Handcraft, Interpersonal, and Technological.

The nine processes work in three general ways to define the content of the curriculum. In grades K–8, they define the content that all students are to be taught. During the Exploration phase in grades 9 and 10, although students remain within all nine processes, they can choose subdivisions of the nine processes for in-depth exploration. During the Selection phase in grades 11 and 12, instructional modules can be developed from specific career entry, continuing college entry, and post secondary entry contents. Each of these contents can then be placed within the appropriate process as an instructional module.

The conceptual framework on which the processes were designed essentially sees the tracks as spirals of evolving skills and abilities, during the years K−10. Initially, the students acquire a skill or new knowledge in the most global context. As they progress, the skills and capabilities are further honed in more complex situations, calling for finer manipulations and applications.

Tracing through one of the processes can serve as a concrete example of the spiral-like evolution of skill and abilities—the Social, Political, and Economic process.

During the K−6 phase, students would be introduced to the basic concepts and methods of looking at man, his past, his culture, and society. They would acquire, in simplest terms, the concepts of society, culture, and political systems. As they move beyond the beginning uses of these concepts, their capabilities would evolve as they confront more sophisticated problems and situations.

More than anything else, the process stresses an orientation rather than a pure category system for nine areas of learning. A pure category system is not possible for several reasons. Learning in certain areas, especially in the sciences and mathematics, has been organized into formal disciplines, and careers are built upon these disciplines. To be a physicist, chemist, or mathematician requires pursuit within the discipline and its organized body of methodology and knowledge. Acquiring cognitive skills that are generic in their application to many contexts constitutes another subdivision of learning processes. Finally, career specific processes—working with tools and machinery and applying various intellectual techniques in a work context—define another grouping of learning processes.

Because we cannot organize the content of the curriculum into homogeneous categories, the nine processes must reflect the differences among different kinds of content the student is to learn. However, the use of the term, process, underscores the need for arranging instructional objectives and methods that allow the student to be an active participant in the learning activity. With the perspective that the term implies, the career context falls in as a matter of course. The things a student learns to do have a real and functional context: what it presently enables him to do and what it will enable him to do in future social roles. Moreover, because of the career context, he continually sees the relationship of people working in various career areas to those skills and knowledges he presently is acquiring.

During grades K−6, the nine processes are combined into six main tracks. Communication and Social, Political and Economic processes are combined into one track. Mathematical, Scientific, and Economic processes are also grouped together into another track. The other four processes are on separate tracks. During grades 7−8, the only grouping is to combine Scientific and Technological processes. During grades 9−10 each process forms its own track.

Each process is seen as containing much of the content that presently is taught in elementary and high schools. Three of them were added to include content from career areas not generally present in elementary schools and the first two years of high school. These are Tool and Handcraft, Interpersonal, and Technological.

The nine processes work in three general ways to define the content of the curriculum. In grades K—8, they define the content that all students are to be taught. During the Exploration phase in grades 9 and 10, although students remain within all nine processes, they can choose subdivisions of the nine processes for in-depth exploration. During the Selection phase in grades 11 and 12, instructional modules can be developed from specific career entry, continuing college entry, and post secondary entry contents. Each of these contents can then be placed within the appropriate process as an instructional module.

The conceptual framework on which the processes were designed essentially sees the tracks as spirals of evolving skills and abilities, during the years K—10. Initially, the students acquire a skill or new knowledge in the most global context. As they progress, the skills and capabilities are further honed in more complex situations, calling for finer manipulations and applications.

Tracing through one of the processes can serve as a concrete example of the spiral-like evolution of skill and abilities—the Social, political, and Economic process.

During the K—6 phase, students would be introduced to the basic concepts and methods of looking at man, his past, his culture, and society. They would acquire, in simplest terms, the concepts of society, culture, and political systems. As they move beyond the beginning uses of these concepts, their capabilities would evolve as they confront more sophisticated problems and situations.

Use of the Nine Processes to
Structure a Curriculum

In grades 7—8, students would be introduced to the social science disciplines of History, Anthropology, Archeology, Sociology, Political Science, and Psychology. Their past investigations—looking at data, comparing and verifying information, interpreting events and behavior—are placed into the confines of an appropriate discipline. At this time, skills used globally at the onset become more specific and tied to the organization and structure of the discipline. They learn that historians use certain conceptual tools in examining the past, while anthropologists, political scientists, and sociologists employ others.

In grades 9—10, students can explore among these disciplines in depth, depending upon their personal interests. They could explore, for example, various careers that use these disciplines as their center.

Use of the Nine Processes to Structure a Curriculum

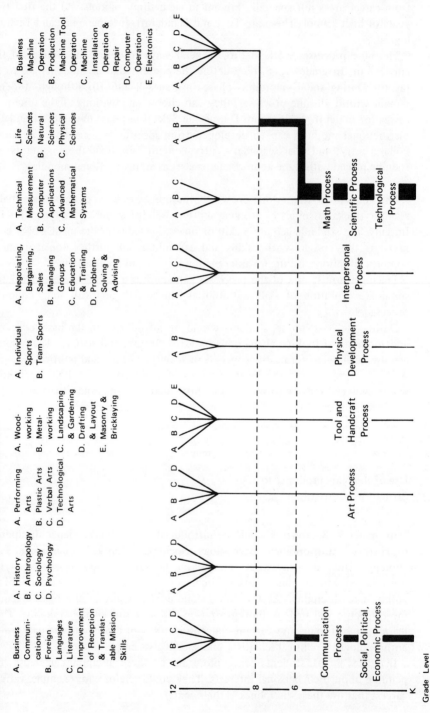

Relation of the Clustering System
To the Nine Processes

A collapsed clustering system is proposed in the Awareness phase, K–6. Occupations are arranged into two groups: those concerned with production of goods, and services. Career levels are placed into two categories: higher and lower.

The clustering system provides a simple context for the learning experiences to be included within the processes. Under artistic processes, for example, working with various media can include simple schemes for introducing artists and general information about their lives and functions. The necessary dimension that the clustering system interjects into the nine processes during the Awareness phase is the general relationship of what is learned to concrete areas of human activity.

At the Orientation level, the clustering system grows in detail. Career status is now divided into three levels and occupations into five broad areas. Building upon the general relationship of careers to the nine processes, learning experiences can now begin to focus the students' personal interests and needs. The clustering system provides a conceptual structure that leads the student to see how the skills and knowledge he is acquiring fit in with demarcated occupations within five broad areas. The learning experiences can lead the student to realize how pursuit of skills and knowledge within the nine processes lead to specific careers in the five areas. The relationship between the clustering system and the processes has not intrinsically changed from the Awareness level. The input is still directed toware guidance and information about career development.

The clustering system is at full bloom at the Exploration phase (9–10). Career levels and areas are placed in a 7 x 12 matrix. Here an additional categorization system is introduced, grouping occupations by broad function. As students choose possible careers, which they will explore in depth, the implications of their choice are fully dimensionalized for them in terms of status, educational requirements, and array of options. Exploration of careers also implies that students will begin to select learning experiences within the processes. To prevent premature choice and later regret, the students should continue to have learning experiences with each process. They can, for example, have the option to explore certain careers in depth within the content of the nine processes.

At this time, the nature of the input that the clustering system makes becomes expanded. While its influence remains tied with guidance and information, the need becomes apparent for arranging exploration experiences so that students can see the implications of selecting among various career options.

During the concluding Selection phase, the student chooses one, or a combination, of the outcomes available to him. In the earlier phases, the input of the clustering system was to help plan learning experiences that would guide and inform the students about the world of work and the many important variables associated with making a career choice. At this point, now that students have made a choice, the clustering system becomes the source of the specific content students need for direct entry to jobs. Additional curriculum contents can be drawn from junior and four-year college entry requirements, and from post-secondary specialized schools, for those students who have chosen careers requiring an education beyond high school.

These contents can be placed in one of the branches of the nine processes, in the form of instructional modules. The arrangement of all contents into modules permit a highly individualized curriculum. Any combination of outcomes can be chosen by a student. One student may want to prepare exclusively for direct entry in several jobs that are unrelated, because they are congruent with his personal interests and talents. Another student may choose to prepare for both college and job entry—college entry because it is the path to a career, job entry because he must work summers and part-time to pay for his education. These are only two of the many possible arrangements of outcomes particular students can choose.

The clustering system during the Selection phase shifts its impact on the education of students. For those students who have chosen direct job entry after high school, instruction has to be provided in the complex of skills and knowledges needed to make entry possible. The usual solution has been to separate those students and place them into a vocational track. The arrangement on the job contents derived from the clustering system into instructional modules permits all students to pursue job entry. It ends the depressing choice students have to make between entrance into one of two tracks, vocational and academic. It also permits students to choose among multiple outcomes and pursue highly individualized courses of study.

Summary

We have recommended the use of nine processes as the means to place instructional content arriving from various sources—basal cognitive skills, job-entry skills, higher educational entry requirements—into a general curriculum model. The use of the term "process" is oriented toward instructional objectives and the arrangement of learning experiences. The learner would acquire skills and capabilities as a result of engagements and confrontations with the learning material. The evolution of the acquisition of skills and capabilities should occur in a spiral arrangement, moving from global to specific, elaborated conceptual systems, and from simple to complex manipulations and applications.

The clustering system serveas as a planning model, integrated with the progression of career development goals: Awareness, Orientation, Exploration, and Selection. The clustering system makes three major inputs into the curriculum model. During the Awareness, Orientation, and Exploration phases, the major inputs are to the functions of information and guidance. The clustering system can serve as the basis for arranging instructional objectives, content, and methods that guide and inform students about the world of work. In the Selection phase, job skills can be derived from the clustering system and, in turn, are translated into instructional modules. These modules can be placed into the appropriate process, together with other modules derived from other contents. Thus, an individualized curriculum can be built where students can prepare for single or multiple outocmes of their own choosing.

The outlines presented in the graphic illustration are general recommendations as to the arrangement and content of the nine processes. They should not be considered definitive and complete in detail. They are offered simply as a take-off point from which to develop a comprehensive model of the curriculum. This process structure takes into account the goals and projected outcomes of the CCEM, and the present organization of schools, and is coordinated with the clustering system.

PART 4

Career Education Systems

Career Education Systems are being designed and developed in both the public and private sectors. Marland's remarks, earlier in this volume, give specific examples, as does the article by Martin.

The total concept of Career Education systems refers not only to a comprehensive instructional design but also to the utilization of the products of this instruction within the labor force. Thus, the emphasis in this section is not on describing operational Career Education systems, *per se*, but rather on providing some positive input into the direction that Career Education systems may have to go and the number of factors that must be considered. Inherently linked with this is a relationship between the working world and the academic world and the exploration of designs for the appropriate training, development, and utilization of manpower.

The first article discusses the elements in building a comprehensive Career Education system. Bruce Reinhart and his co-authors look at all aspects of the systems approach, place heavy emphasis on the personal individual factors and give specific examples. Alternate examples of operational systems may be found in the articles of Nolan Estes, Marie Y. Martin, and John Grede, who discusses the post-secondary Career Education system.

Richard F. Peter discusses the American Industry Program as an integrating force for making realistic career choices and Elmer Winter offers suggestions for the systematic development of Career Education as a partnership between business and the school. Louis W. Bender takes this one step further as he reports on middle manpower utilization through Career Education.

Bruce Reinhart, Neill Slack,
and David Buettner

BUILDING A
COMPREHENSIVE
EDUCATION SYSTEM*

At the Center for Vocational and Technical Education (CVTE) at Ohio State University, people from every sector of the educational community are working on the conceptualization of career education. Restructuring education around a career development theory requires a detailed framework for constructing career education curriculums, and curriculum components must be appropriately selected to assure that the program is comprehensive and soundly based.

The identification and definition of the elements and outcomes used by CVTE were achieved by examining and integrating the work of many people in the fields of human growth and development, vocational guidance, and curriculum development. The Career Education Matrix as shown in the graphic illustration following, contains the basic elements on the left side, essential outcomes on the right side, and years of schooling in the center.

Career Education Matrix

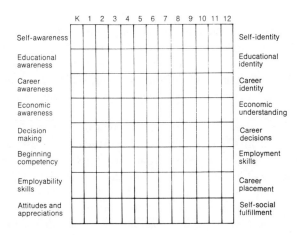

*Bruce Reinhart, Neill Slack, and David Buettner—"Building a Comprehensive Career Education System" reprinted from the April, 1973 issue of *School Shop* copyright 1973 by Prakken Publications, Inc.

135

This matrix was based on the assumption that it is essential that each person know himself and develop a personal value system; perceive the relationship between education and life roles; acquire knowledge of the wide range of careers; be able to perceive processes in production, distribution, and consumption relative to his economic environment; be able to use information in determining alternatives and reaching decisions; acquire and develop skills which are viewed as ways that man extends his behavior; develop social and communication skills appropriate to career placement and adjustment; and develop appropriate feelings toward himself and others. Building on this framework, the CVTE staff went on to identify goals and performance objectives appropriate for each of the 104 cells in the matrix grid.

Career Guidance

The career education movement is indebted to counseling and guidance, and industrial educators will need to understand more about these areas. The following provisions will be incorporated in The Comprehensive Career Education Model (CCEM): Teachers, counselors, and others will work as a team in dealing with students, parents, instruction, planning, and evaluation. Critical transitions and decision and action points have been identified throughout the K-12 developmental sequence for students, and industrial educators will assist students in moving smoothly through grade levels, training programs, and developmental problems. Each curriculum unit being developed has career guidance implications which will be specified in the teaching materials. There will be extensive staff development for all personnel—counselors, teachers, administrators, and others—and all will have a larger guidance responsibility.

Another requirement for successfully establishing a comprehensive career education system at the local level is the development and utilization of a number of supporting information systems. Reliable information must be gathered, stored, analyzed, and disseminated to meet the needs of many participants throughout the district, and information pertaining to individual students will be needed to help them plan their educational experiences and help the staff evaluate their programs.

The top priority in the support system component of the CCEM has been to develop the Career Information System (CIS). Although the CIS does not solve the problem of clustering occupations in the simple, popular sense, it does provide a structure of knowledge about work that integrates a number of clustering systems, and also includes product information (clusters), process information (occupations), and personal information (worker traits).

The career education movement has emerged when the clamor for more community involvement and authority for education is increasing. There is a growing belief that the consumers of schooling—parents, students, the poor and socially disenfranchised, employers, and taxpayers—as well as teachers and administrators, should share the decision-making responsibilities. Developing this role will be a monumental task, but educators must respond to the legitimate demands of the community to share in the education process.

Career Curriculums

The headlong rush to install career curriculums is a grave concern. Most of the current curriculums that have been assessed are mediocre or poor, and there is no evidence that they fulfill their claims. A sound management of curriculum development is crucial or the entire career education movement will be jeopardized.

The occupational exploration component of the CCEM is designed to provide an overview of the world of work based on the student's occupational awareness experiences in grades 4 through 6, and additional experiences that will facilitate further career development, specifically, an increase in career decision-making ability.

A portion of this component to be offered at grades 7 through 9 is organized into 12 occupational clusters. Orientation experiences in these clusters is initated in 7th grade. If the student desires continued study in a cluster, exploration experiences are provided in grades 8 and 9. The development of a sound and personal experience base is the aim of exploration. Each cluster is divided into several segments, and each segment into three types of modules: simulation, occupational information, and community involvement. Following are examples of simulation modules in several selected clusters

Natural Resources
   Agriculture (growing and/or raising replenishable resources)
   Extraction (removing nonreplenishable resources)
   Environmental Protection
   Land Use Planning
   Recreational Use of Natural Resources

Manufacturing
   Research and Development
   Product Design
   Production Planning
   Production
   Consumer Protection

Construction
   Planning Construction Projects
   Organizing to Build
   Preparing the Site
   Building Structures

Trade/Finance
  Stock Market
  Banking
  Wholesale Trade
  Retail Trade

Simulation modules get students involved in work-like situations, but do not provide them with a depth of knowledge in areas such as characteristics of workers, entry requirements, employment outlook, and rewards. Such information will only be relevant to students if they become interested in an occupation, however, and is available as needed.

A community involvement module is needed to assist students in relating their simulation experiences and associated occupational information to the world outside the school building. This module should accompany each simulation module and include a variety of methods for enhancing the realism of the simulation module (work experience, directed observation, field trips, industrial speakers, etc.).

A priority of the 7 through 9 curriculum component has been the development of a comprehensive set of guidelines, accompanied by a sample cluster segment, to assist persons involved in developing an exploration component in career education. These guidelines have been developed around concerns to articulate with existing K–6 career awareness level curriculums; to insure that all possible instruction is learner-centered; to adopt a clustering concept that helps assure exploration, flexibility, career development, and decision-making, and provides occupational information; to involve the community; and to use simulation activities whenever possible for in-school programs.

The 10–12 curriculum, the career preparation component, is a culminating effort to prepare students for entry into a postsecondary work or educational experience. This curriculum must reach the entire high-school population, and is designed to move each student as far as possible in his career development. For some this can best be achieved by learning how to perform the tasks required in a particular area or occupation. Such an activity has two key outcomes—a salable skill, and an expanded base of experience on which better career decisions can be made.

From many methods of providing an effective career preparation program, the CCEM has identified three major categories; alternatives to the subject-based curriculum, clustering concepts, and refined and extended vocational-education programs.

Alternatives Advocated

Alternatives to a subject-based curriculum are advocated by many educators on the basis that curriculum should go beyond the constraints of a subject area and directly address the needs and desires of the students. While the CCEM is carefully considering alternatives—which develop desirable characteristics and capabilities of students. yet are devoid of subject matter area constraints—for future research and development, the nature and past operation of the CCEM project are not well adapted to such an undertaking.

The cluster concept is especially useful for students without a specific career interest or choice. It has become a valuable concept for career educators, and the career preparation component of the CCEM recognizes the need for including an effective cluster concept in a comprehensive 10—12 career preparation program.

The 1968 National Advisory Council on Vocational Education found that vocational education was effective but did not reach many students who needed it, and that the transition from vocational education to work could be improved if schools assumed greater responsibility for helping students to find jobs and succeed in them. The CCEM staff is presently developing and testing vocational-like curriculum units which would build on the experinece of past curriculums and would be successful in placing a student's vocational preparation into a career development perspective; enabling students to find, apply for, and succeed on jobs; and reaching a larger portion of high-school students with an expanded offering of occupationally related programs.

Flexible delivery systems are a key in development of the curriculum units. They will be installable as either a cooperative education program, a community-school approach, or a scheduled or nonscheduled in-school program.

A comprehensive 10—12 component should:

Articulate with the 7—9 career exploration phase and continue the options to investigate and explore a variety of occupations.

Provide job-entry skills for those who have made a firm career decision.

Continue to actively involve the industrial community.

Provide instruction that is individualized, student-centered, modular, or packaged whenever feasible.

We have described only a few salient features of the evolving CCEM. As career education matures, complete guidelines will be available for practitioners, but industrial educators must now assume the responsibility of testing the concepts in the practical laboratories of the classroom and the shop.

Richard F. Peter

AMERICAN INDUSTRY
PROGRAM*

"I can't find a job . . . !"
"I'm in a boring, dead-end job with no place to go . . . !"
The message of frustration from unemployed and unhappy workers is loud and clear: our society can no longer tolerate an educational system which largely ignores the world of work and the real-life problems associated with earning a living in meaningful careers.

The career education concept challenges all educators to work together toward a solution to the career education problem. The objective is a blend of students and curriculums in which academic preparation and vocational-career preparation are fused into a single strong system that will achieve maximum placement of high-school graduates.

The American Industry Program (AIP) is playing a significant role in providing an integrating force for making realistic career choices that is now lacking in traditional school programs. The program was developed at the University of Wisconsin-Stout with grant support from the Ford Foundation and the U.S. Office of Education. One of its main objectives is to provide students with a broad understanding of industry so that career decisions may be made in the light of hands-on experiences in a wide variety of jobs.

A Conceptual Structure of the
Knowledges Necessary to Understand
American Industry

Conceptual Areas

The structuring of content to provide students with this broad view of industry was accomplished by identifying 13 conceptual areas which apply to any and all industry. (Fig. 1). This structure establishes a framework for studying each conceptual area in relationship to every other area and to the whole of industry. The lines connecting the concepts illustrate the fact that each body of know-

---

*Richard F. Peter—"American Industry Program" reprinted with permission from the April, 1973 issue of *School Shop* copyright 1973 by Prakken Publications, Inc.

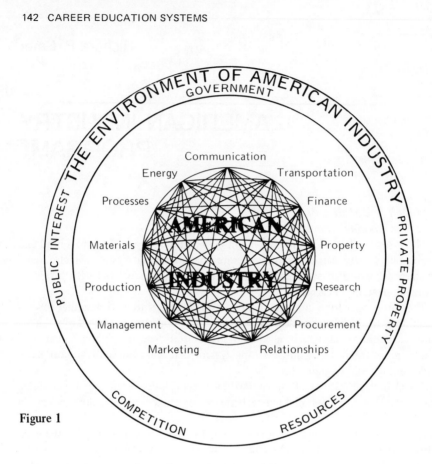

Figure 1

ledge is related to and should be studied in conjunction with every other area. This reflects a true industrial organization in which, for example, management must be concerned with every other aspect of the enterprise: communications, transportation, finance, marketing, etc., and vice versa.

The AIP structure also illustrates that industry is affected by the environment in which it operates. Five major facets of the American environment are studied, namely: public interest, government, private property, resources, and competition. Each influences the way in which industry operates in the United States and distinguishes American industry from industry in other countries throughout the world.

The American Industry Program operates at three levels: junior high (Level I), 9th or 10th grade (Level II), and 12th grade (Level III). Instructor's guides, student booklets, and a variety of audiovisual materials have been developed and field tested. Level I has received the widest distribution, and is being taught in all types of schools across the country.

In most cases AIP is taught in conjunction with traditional offerings in industrial arts. However, this article will attempt to point out unique features of the program which allow it to be incorporated into a variety of K–12 career education programs.

Figure 2   LEVEL I – AMERICAN INDUSTRY COURSE OUTLINE
TEACHER DIRECTED

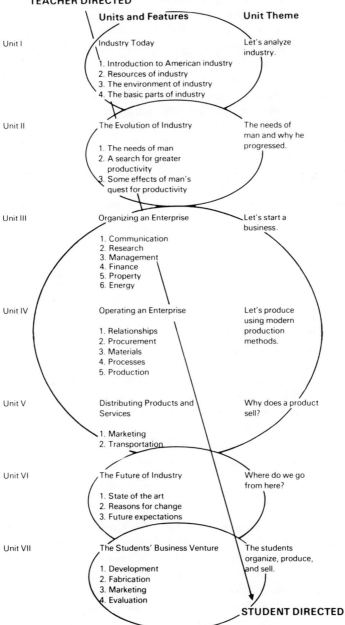

	Units and Features	Unit Theme
Unit I	Industry Today 1. Introduction to American industry 2. Resources of industry 3. The environment of industry 4. The basic parts of industry	Let's analyze industry.
Unit II	The Evolution of Industry 1. The needs of man 2. A search for greater productivity 3. Some effects of man's quest for productivity	The needs of man and why he progressed.
Unit III	Organizing an Enterprise 1. Communication 2. Research 3. Management 4. Finance 5. Property 6. Energy	Let's start a business.
Unit IV	Operating an Enterprise 1. Relationships 2. Procurement 3. Materials 4. Processes 5. Production	Let's produce using modern production methods.
Unit V	Distributing Products and Services 1. Marketing 2. Transportation	Why does a product sell?
Unit VI	The Future of Industry 1. State of the art 2. Reasons for change 3. Future expectations	Where do we go from here?
Unit VII	The Students' Business Venture 1. Development 2. Fabrication 3. Marketing 4. Evaluation	The students organize, produce, and sell.

STUDENT DIRECTED

Classroom Activities

In Level I, junior-high-school students are exposed to an overall view of industry through a brief study of the 13 conceptual areas (Fig. 2). Students gain first-hand experience in solving problems related to industry. They begin by participating in a teacher-directed enterprise in which a product or service is produced and distributed. This provides a basis for discussion of real-life applications of the conceptual areas. The management aspects of an industrial organization are enthusiastically studied by the students who might otherwise be "turned off" by such academically oriented topics as "research and development", "communications", "finance", "procurement", "energy", etc.

As the class proceeds, the students begin to organize their own enterprise, with the instructor acting as a consultant. Students develop product ideas into prototypes and compete for the company contract to produce the item or service. A corporation is formed and management begins to recruit, hire, and train student employees who apply for the various job openings. Students are hired in a real-life atmosphere of job applications, interviews, and orientation sessions. Management selects employees on the basis of interests, aptitudes, and previous work experience. The employees decide whether to negotiate individually with the employer or to form a union to negotiate a work contract.

As tooling up for production continues, students are actively engaged in a variety of tasks that must be efficiently coordinated if the company is to turn a profit in a highly competitive market. Students learn to analyze new situations and to solve problems, using management, production, or marketing techniques that are relevant to today's advanced technologies in these areas.

Level II has been developed to expand the students' understanding of the concepts of American industry and to increase their ability to identify logical relationships among the concepts. The areas of company development, product development, and marketing give students in-depth experiences which utilize knowledge of all conceptual areas to develop an efficient enterprise. The experience gained in Level I allows students of Level II to establish and operate an enterprise which incorporates more complex and sophisticated industrial techniques for producing goods and services.

Level III allows students to explore any idea of industry in depth. They may choose topics of interest and develop knowledge and skill in these areas through a system of independent study. Self-directed study and work are emphasized at this level.

The concept of self-awareness is carefully developed in all three levels as students interact with each other in large and small groups within the enterprise. Each student is given an opportunity to experience management functions as well as worker functions in a broad spectrum of jobs. American Industry classes organize as many as three or four separate enterprises to produce goods and services throughout the school year. In each case, job applications are filled out, interviews are conducted, fringe benefits are negotiated, and a training center is established to prepare each employee for his job. Students determine desirable characteristics found in successful workers in management, production, and marketing areas of the enterprise. Checklists are developed for studying an occupation in terms of qualifications, skills, and knowledge required, working conditions, benefits, and the advantages and disadvantages of various occupations. Role playing, therefore, as an integral part of the program, encourages students to investigate and evaluate their abilities, potentialities, and attitudes toward a broad spectrum of careers.

Learning by Concept

The three levels of AIP have been designed to incorporate the principles Asahel Woodruff formulated regarding conceptual learning. Concepts of industry are identified, discussed, and applied to realistic industrial situations. Students learn to analyze problems from a conceptual viewpoint to determine commonalities and relationships which can be applied to new situations as they arise. Students are encouraged to be creative, flexible, and adaptable in their work. Conceptual learning helps students to see relationships between the job they are doing and other activities within the enterprise. Students may be transferred from one job to another as the need arises. This experience, with lateral and vertical movement within an organization, can prove invaluable to the student in maintaining his employability in the world of work.

An encouraging result of the career education movement thus far is that many teachers are becoming aware that career education is the collective responsibility of the entire educational system. In the past, the burden of career education has rested almost entirely on the shoulders of our industrial-arts and vocational-education teachers. Now, at long last, educators are beginning to realize that education for a career means education of the whole person; that math, science, social studies, and all other teachers have vital roles to play in the career education continuum.

However, the pressing problem here is not a question of convincing teachers that they should relate their subject matter to the world of work. Most teachers are eager to participate. The problem arises from the fact that, as a group, teachers' experiences have been mostly in the field of education, so many lack technical literacy and a comprehensive understanding of the world of industry. The result is that teachers are experiencing considerable difficulty in designing their own career education programs to truly reflect the world of work. Those who do succeed are faced with the problem of integrating their efforts with a total school approach toward a comprehensive career education program.

Interdisciplinary Approach

The conceptual structure of AIP illustrates that the world of industry must draw on a broad spectrum of interrelated and interdependent bodies of knowledge if it is to function efficiently. These 13 conceptual areas identified by AIP cut across the various disciplines now taught in the school curriculum and provide opportunity for team teaching and interdisciplinary classes.

A typical example of an interdisciplinary effort is taking place at Hohokam Elementary in Scottsdale, Arizona. Here 7th-grade students are engaged in an AIP enterprise in which careers are studied as companies are formed to design, produce, and market a variety of products and services. All 7th-grade teachers are involved in the program, and each academic area contributes to the development of industrial concepts related to the discipline.

For example, the principles of management, company organization, government controls, and other related topics are treated in the social studies classes. Communications and advertising are taught in the language arts area. Math classes compute costs, maintain financial records, and determine break-even points for selling prices, expenses, and profits. The industrial-arts teacher provides assistance in engineering and organizing production processes. The science areas help with research and development.

In some cases, students rent space and equipment from the school and subcontract the production of components for their enterprise to other classes in the school. Teachers are hired to act as consultants when difficult problems arise. In this type of environment, students begin to see the relevance of class activities to the world of work, and they gain practical experience in applying their knowledge and skills to real-life problems.

The interdisciplinary approach to studying industry accomplishes several critical goals: 1) it provides students with real-life experiences in a variety of careers; 2) academic and industrial-arts subjects are fused into an integrated curriculum of career education; and 3) both students and teachers gain insight into the complex structure of industry.

For the students, it provides an optimal background for making career choices. For teachers, it provides an enlightening experience with those common elements which apply to any industry. Hence, the task of relating all subject areas to the world of work is simplified as career education becomes a total school effort.

Enthusiastic Response

The enthusiastic response of students, teachers, and parents of Scottsdale and other communities to this exciting new program is living testimony of its worth as a career-education program.

The industrial-arts teacher who may not be able to involve the whole school in AIP enterprises may still utilize the expertise of other teachers in carrying out his program. Figure 3 illustrates the relationship of AIP concept areas to other subjects in the school. Experts from the community may also be brought in to discuss certain topics with the students and to relate the student enterprise to local industry.

Besides being interdisciplinary, a truly effective career education program requires a continuing effort throughout K–12 and beyond. An articulated program should first provide the widest possible understanding of industry as a basis for career choice. Once a basic understanding has been attained, a study of occupational clusters can help students begin to narrow their career choices. As choices are further narrowed, specific skill and technology oriented courses should be available for developing job-entry skills.

AMERICAN INDUSTRY CONCEPTS	RELATED SUBJECTS
Government—Public interest Relationships—Private property Resources—Competition	Social studies, Geography
Communications	English, Speech, Science
Marketing—Transportation Finance—Procurement Management—Property	Distributive education, Business education, Mathematics
Research—Energy Processes—Materials	Science, Mathematics, Art Home economics
Production—Processes Materials	Vocational education, Home economics, Industrial arts

Figure 3

This phase of the program might take place at the end of high school, in a technical school, or perhaps in college depending on the type of preparation needed for the career that is chosen (Fig. 4). This illustration also points out that "a job" is not necessarily "a career" and that career education is a life-long process that does not end with graduation.

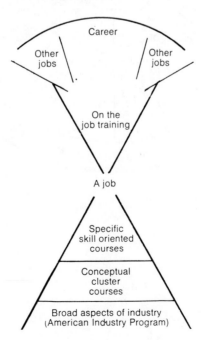

Figure 4

The American Industry Program fits easily into such an articulated program. Figure 5 illustrates how the conceptual areas studied as a whole in Levels I and II provide a natural transition to the study of clusters, such as communications, materials and processes, power and energy, etc. These clusters in turn, lead to the study of specific areas of concentration related to that cluster. Finally, job entry can be accomplished in occupational clusters appearing in the outer circle of the illustration.

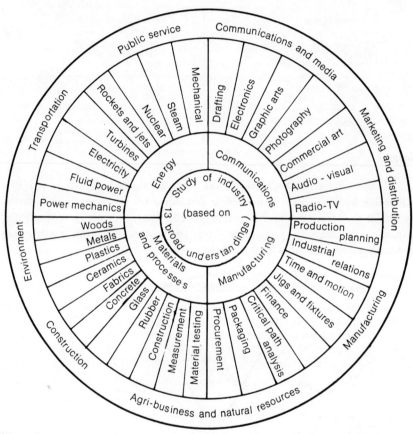

Figure 5

Elmer Winter

CAREER EDUCATION—A PARTNERSHIP BETWEEN BUSINESS AND THE SCHOOL*

I am very happy to be with you today to share some thoughts that I think, as a businessman, might be useful to you in this Conference. As a businessman, I have had considerable opportunity over the years to be rather heavily involved and deeply concerned in the entire subject of career education. In my work I have occasion to meet with many businessmen throughout the United States, and in our discussions we frequently get to the question of the need for more trained people in industry. We refer particularly to the problems of finding a sufficient number of trained young people to fill our job requirements.

Several of us from the business community were asked a few years ago to prepare papers for a conference at Princeton, relating to the closing of the gap between education and the job. In the paper that I presented, I stated that no useful purpose would be served by attempting to lay blame for the inadequacies of our educational system in the past. I tried to point out new ideas which could be explored to provide greater employability of youth.

I still believe that your time at this Conference would be best spent in trying not to place what I refer to as the blame for our past failures, but to rather try to think a plan creatively to take care of the needs of our youth and our employers for tomorrow.

I would like to issue some challenges to you today that I would hope might well form the basis of some of your discussions and planning. My challenges to you would be as follows:

First, we must recognize that the majority of jobs in years ahead will not require a college education. The United States Office of Education estimates that 4 out of 5 jobs, or 80 percent of the jobs created in the decade of the 70's, will require vocational or technical training but not a college diploma.

It may surprise you, as it did me, that the majority of these jobs will compete with college graduate degree jobs in terms of starting salary, advancement and salary potential. And more importantly, in many cases they will offer more

---

*Elmer Winter—"Career Education—A Partnership Between Business and the School" reprinted from the June 15th, 1973 issue of *Vital Speeches of the Day* by permission of the author.

personal job satisfaction and contribute as much or more to society than many of the routine jobs requiring a college degree.

The second challenge that I would suggest to you is we must update the teaching curriculum in all technical fields. Nearly 60 percent of the products to be made in the 1970's had not even been invented in 1969. Think of what this means in terms of updating teaching curriculum and think of what it will take on the part of ALL of us here today to keep education current in view of the accelerating pace we face today and tomorrow.

Perhaps the career education job that we must do together is best illustrated by a recent statement from the U.S. Department of Labor. It pointed out the fact that by the year 2000—only 27 years from now—two thirds of today's kindergarten students will fill jobs which don't even exist today—jobs which haven't even been "invented" yet. If the year 2000 is too far off for you to worry about today and tomorrow, how about the year 1980—that's only 7 years away. The U.S. Department of Labor says that 30,000 types of jobs will be available in 1980, as opposed to the 21,000 types of jobs that exist today. We need to come up with extensive plans as to how we will develop the necessary curriculum in our schools that will prepare our youth for these 30,000 types of jobs that will be available in 1980.

Third, we need to change the attitudes of parents towards career education. As teachers, businessmen, guidance counselors, parents, taxpayers—and as just plain American citizens—we have all helped to convince an entire generation of children—our own children—that the *only* first class citizens in the United States are college graduates. And we have done this in spite of the fact that half—that's half—of those who enter college, drop out. Yes, in spite of the fact that only 17 percent of those entering the labor force today need a four year college education as a prerequisite to employment, we have told today's children that they are second class citizens if they have "ONLY" a vocational or technical education.

The economic, the social and even the political implications of this national brainwashing campaign which all of us have conducted on our children are truly enormous. If you will, consider these current problems and how they might be related to what we have made our children believe.

Consider the number of unemployed scientists and engineers—including Ph.D's—in today's labor market.

Consider the fact that in June of 1972, 234,000 school teachers graduated from college to compete for about 116,000 teaching jobs.

Think about the number of private colleges and universities—including Harvard and Yale—whose current expenses exceed their income.

Consider the fact that high school graduates, who follow college preparatory courses in high school, but do not go on to college, enter the labor market today directly from high school as essentially unskilled workers—at a time when unskilled jobs are virtually nonexistent in metropolitan labor markets throughout the country.

Remember too, that the 50 percent of students entering college only to drop out before graduation, are also basically unprepared to enter the labor market because they have no marketable skills.

Consider also the fact that each year, a rising surplus of college graduates are competing for a declining number of jobs requiring a college degree.

While we need scientists and engineers who are college trained, we must recognize for each scientist or engineer there are at least a half dozen or more technicians and craftsmen needed to carry on work which is as important as that of the man or woman who thought up the idea. The men or women who build, test, try out, adjust and repair the equipment are, in my opinion, as vital in our industrial economy as the engineer and the scientist.

Fourth, we need to bring the business community into the planning of the educational system. I believe that industry should invest the necessary resources as well as the time and personnel to help our educators design effective programs which will make our young people more employable. The businessman should be a key element in the educational picture. He is in a position to know what the skilled manpower requirements will be for the next five years—the next ten years, and he can make an important contribution to our educational processes if he participates in curriculum planning and helps establish the thrust of our vocational training.

We have work-study programs. They are very effective. We need more. The primary objectives for high school work experience should be:

the promotion of good student attitudes toward work;
the promotion of good individual work habits;
the encouragement of desirable traits of character;
the promotion of feelings of self-respect and achievement in students;
the promotion of cooperative attitudes in students;
the promotion of student guidance, including some vocational preparation;
making possible a limited supervised introduction of students to the activities
   and demands of the normal work world.

There are many advantages to employers in participating in cooperative work-study programs. They provide employers with:

a reliable source of better trained, more experienced help;
affords a better acquaintance with prospective employees of the community;
encourages employers to take an active part in the school program and enables
   them to become partners with the school in the educative process;
reduces labor turnover;
provides employers with a steady source of trained help for peak periods;
enables other potential employees to see the advantages of training before
   graduation.

Hopefully at this Conference methods will be designed to meet the challenge of expanding work-study programs.

Fifth, Industry must help develop a better awareness on the part of guidance counselors as to changing job needs. With the rapid changes that are taking place in technology, greater emphasis must be placed upon providing our school counselors with information on jobs, new requirements, availability, salary or wage scales, and opportunities for promotion. This will enable the high school counselor to make an important effort to bridge the gap between student interest in a vocation and actual entry into vocational work. Detailed information about jobs should be made as available to any student in high school and college as any other source of reference in the library.

We need to develop programs which will provide schools with information, personnel films and film slides, in-plant visitations, resource materials from private corporation libraries, and other aids to instruction. Business organizations will gladly assist school counselors so that there is a greater awareness of the changing job requirements and opportunities for employment in a community.

Workshops and seminars for counselors and school personnel in placement and vocational training should be jointly developed by the school staff and industry. Directors of training in a business community should be given the opportunity to present their needs in terms of qualifications for various jobs. Schools are sometimes accused of educating for the job that is no longer in demand. New jobs and new processes as a result of industrial research are being created. Cooperation with industry is essential so that our schools will be conversant with the very latest jobs and techniques.

Sixth, Industry must provide faculty to technical schools. While it may mean a sacrifice to make industry personnel available to schools, in the long run business and industry will come out ahead. They will be able to employ graduates of technical schools trained by their own people. Business frequently retires men with exceptional skills and knowledge at a fairly early age. The so-called "senior citizen" in retirement puts a lot of production skill on the shelf. Most of these men have many skills which could be shared with the youth in the vocational schools and technical institutes. Many schools are looking for men with these skills.

It would be helpful if business and industry would consider retiring men early or releasing them several hours a week on the condition that they would take a position teaching in a vocational or technical institute. In this way, there would be a greater contribution to the realistic preparation of youth and adults for the work force.

Industry should also make available to vocational schools members who will serve on advisory boards. In a recent survey, which we made in our company, Manpower, Inc., of personnel directors across the country, 22 indicated that they serve on an advisory board at their vocational school, and 89 indicated that they do not. In answer to the question as to whether they would be willing to serve, 64 replied 'yes' and 50 said 'no.'

I believe the business community is waiting to be asked and would be of great assistance in providing members of their staff as teachers and as advisors.

Seventh, we must design new ways of breaking up jobs into trainable separate components. There are many jobs that exist today that can be divided up so that portions of the job can be done by people with considerably less training. This can apply to the fields of engineering, accounting, law and many others.

Working with the bar association or accounting society, for example, jobs can be divided so that there will be opportunities for young people to take training where lawyer skills are required to assist the lawyer, or the accountant. In this area, as I see it, there are many new opportunities to break out of traditional patterns and offer new skills training to our young people.

Eighth, the schools and business must play a greater role in the training of our young people in correctional institutions. I believe that there is a great area of neglect that we ought to be examining and take positive steps to correct. I am thinking in terms of the large numbers of young people who are in our penal institutions and who are not getting the training that will permit them to get back into the work force when they are released.

I had occasion to examine some of the courses that are given to young people in these correctional institutions. In my opinion, many of them fall way short of what is needed to make these young people employable when they serve out their term. Some of these courses are obsolete, the equipment that is used is obsolete, and there is not sufficient motivation to encourage these young people to get the type of training that they need for jobs that they will be seeking when they leave the institution. This represents a tremendous waste of talent of young people, which must be corrected through joint effort by the schools, business and the correctional institutions. I would hope that this Conference could address itself to this problem.

Our company recently conducted a survey through our Manpower Research Council on the subject of "Employability of Youth." We asked 400 companies throughout the United States about their attitudes on the employability of youth. I am sure that you will be interested in the answers that were provided by these companies that employed more than 650,000 people.

94.5 percent reported that the young people they are hiring readily accept training. Doesn't this tell you something? Doesn't this say that if the training is available, young people will readily accept it?

For those who had apprenticeship programs, a substantial number believed that these programs could be improved if the following were to take place:

Shortening the length of time required in apprenticeship—four years is unrealistically long for some skills.
More vocational counseling is necessary for the student not planning on college.
Offer improved job-related training in high school and vocational schools.
Give high school students better exposure to vocational opportunities.
Make it possible for more young people to enter apprenticeship programs.

You might be interested in knowing how those surveys across the country regarded the training provided by vocational schools: 27.2 percent believed that the training was very good; 51.5 percent believed it was good; and 21.3 percent believed that it was only fair.

When asked how vocational schools could do a better job, the suggestions most frequently listed were:

Give more general job orientation to those who will enter at lower skill levels.
Keep more abreast of needs and requirements of local business and industry. Then gear the training and counseling efforts to those needs.
Teach skills that are more current and that have a future.
Establish a better liaison with the companies which will be hiring the school's graduates.
Institute more work-study programs, include industry representatives on advisory boards and update classroom materials more frequently.

When asked the question, "Do you believe guidance counselors have a good understanding of our future employment needs?", 48.4 percent said 'yes'; 51.6 percent said 'no.' Again this would indicate the need for a much closer working relationship between industry and the educational institutions.

The success of any community—whether it's a community the size of Waterford, or Milwaukee, or even an entire state—is measured largely in terms of its economy. And any community economy is affected primarily by the number of companies which decide to locate or expand within that community. In working with the heads of other companies, I've learned, as I am sure you have, that in looking for new plant sites, one of the company's major locational considerations is whether an area has a well trained and educated labor force and an educational system that can upgrade that labor force to meet changing industry needs. A company's management has to be sure that its community has an educational system able to roll with the technological punches. Without this type of educational system, industries can't possible fill their human resource needs. And while natural resources can be shipped in from out of state, human resources are much more difficult to come by.

So without the necessary partnerships which will keep education from becoming stagnant in a community, the costs to industry and the whole community can be great.

Now, I've heard businessmen say that their company just doesn't have the time or the budget to spend on involving itself in educational problems. I am sure that almost every educator here today has heard or read of some businessman or woman who had the attitude that "the problems of education should be solved by the educator—business has its own problems to solve, not the least of which is operating within the budget."

Well, that businessman might be surprised to learn that last year alone, business and industry spent almost 15 billion—that's *Billion* dollars—for manpower training and re-education programs for their employees. I ask you, wouldn't it make sense for business to invest some of its time and whatever resources it could in working together with educators in developing partnerships that would result in business having to spend less than 15 billion dollars each year on training or retraining the people it hires?

Wouldn't our state become a much more desirable place for industry to locate and expand if we could point to a healthy partnership between business, industry, and education in Wisconsin? A partnership which would make education an even more effective tool of economic and personal development with each passing year? Partnerships in career education can become one of our most important ways of affecting our community's future.

In this partnership, we have to make certain that tomorrow's students are introduced to ALL of the career opportunities and types of advanced training available to them. As most theorists agree, this career introduction process must be an on-going process, throughout a child's educational experience. A single day or even a junior or senior year devoted to "career orientation" is hardly enough to give a student sufficient time to consider what will bring him or her the greatest satisfaction.

Hopefully, as a result of this Conference, industry and education might develop a "Time Bank" to which business will pledge contributions of time each year. Educators, in need of resource from business, will draw upon the "Time Bank" for whatever services may be needed, whether it be in the areas of teaching or serving on advisory committees.

Looking out into the furure, we may well be able to see new partnerships formed like "Schools without Walls" through which students will be able to spend more time learning about career opportunities through observing and working with those already employed in the field being considered. Through such programs, students will be able to try jobs on for size before they make a commitment to something they don't really understand.

We have a fine educational system in this community. It is certainly one of the key elements responsible for the over-all high standard of living we have achieved today. But the time has come for business and industry to provide more effective support in order to help education meet the tremendous challenge of providing workers to handle the vastly changed jobs of tomorrow's work force.

It is the time that we realize that in our democratic system each individual, as well as the corporation, has an obligation to participate actively in matters relating to education. We must lay the plans in our discussions today and tomorrow to pool the expertise of the business, labor and education representatives at this Conference.

The start which we make through this Conference on new partnerships must be continued in communities across our State. Only if we continue what we start here today does this Conference have the potential for helping us develop the partnerships which we must develop across Wisconsin if our state is to retain a strong and healthy economy, and if our young people are to make successful transitions to satisfying work experiences in our communities.

Louis W. Bender

MIDDLE MANPOWER
UTILIZATION THROUGH
CAREER EDUCATION*

A distinguishing characteristic of contemporary living is the dynamic of change which has led to the concept of "future shock". This phenomenon occurred with sudden reality for many two year colleges when examining the enrollment patterns for the 1972–73 academic year. Overshadowing, perhaps, the problem of over-projections of new enrollees was the dramatic shift towards increased demands for admission to occupational programs, while application for academic transfer programs decreased. It appears the societal change called for by Grant Venn only a few years ago has come to pass:

> Vocational and technical education cannot achieve status auto-
> matically. Education, government, and society as a whole will have
> to gain a better understanding of occupational education and of its
> value to the individual and the nation before this branch of learning
> can acquire the prestige to enroll the number and the kind of stu-
> dents who need it.

Much has been written concerning the responsibility of education to play a major role in raising social attitudes which recognize the dignity of honest labor, regardless of level or type, and to develop relevant programs for an individual to prepare oneself for an occupation.

Many can take credit for contributing to the present status of occupational education. The American Association of Community and Junior Colleges, supported by the W. K. Kellogg Foundation, gave national leadership during the 1960's in fostering the future importance of occupational education and in assisting two-year institutions to develop more appropriate or new innovative training programs for technical, paraprofessional, and midmanagement personnel representing the middle manpower spectrum. Activities by the AACJC ranged from programs designed to gain greater public understanding to curriculum guides to aid instructional personnel.

A growing number of states have contributed to the phenomenon by including

---

*Louis W. Bender–"Middle Manpower Utilization Through Career Education" reprinted with permission from the May, 1973 issue of *Community and Junior College Journal* published by the American Association of Community and Junior Colleges.

postsecondary occupational education goals in recent state master plans. More direct state advocacy can be seen in special state funding formulas or incentives to encourage local institutions to develop more and better occupational programs.

Locally, many educational leaders have championed greater awareness and status for occupational education. Efforts within and without the institutions have been made through a variety of techniques and delivery systems.

The Problem

As desirable as these circumstances might be, a major problem will soon confront us unless something is done about the other side of the coin. Often, little or no work has been done by employers toward proper utilization and recognition of middle manpower personnel.

The paradox now exists that the public is supporting a spectacular growth of area vocational-technical centers and two-year colleges with a specific charge that they emphasize occupational programs, while at the same time the public often ignores opportunities to use their graduates.

Few governmental agencies have taken significant steps to use the products of these institutions. Many personnel directors have made little effort to establish differentiated career tracks taking advantage of postsecondary occupational programs of varying lengths of time.

An example can readily be seen by examining the job descriptions and career classifications at local and state government agencies. Typically, there are only two major entry levels, the high school diploma and the baccalaureate degree. Testimony that this problem exists at the federal level as well could be seen in the *AACJC Governmental Affairs Special* of October 27, 1972, which reported efforts of AACJC to win alternatives to federal personnel policies. That report observed:

> The four-year degree has gained broad recognition as a federal employment standard. The two-year degree enjoys no such recognition. In program support the federal government now gives broad recognition to the community colleges and their growing importance to national manpower goals and development—but there is no parallel recognition in federal hiring.

AACJC Commission on Governmental Affairs felt concerned enough about the problem, in fact, that it adopted a resolution at the association's 1973 convention calling for revision of federal employment standards, for recognition of both the two-year college graduate and student for job entry at appropriate levels, and for wider participation in the cooperative education programs in government.

Analysis of governmental levels identifies the area for greatest need. The AACJC monograph *Government Careers and the Community College* by Andrew

S. Korim describes a variety of public service fields for which local and munic-
ipal civil or career service classifications have been developed.

Examples are given in his monograph of newly emerging middle manpower
fields which are often popular because of close cooperation between the producer (the institution) and the user (the employer) in the formulation of the
curriculum and entry-level provisions, including appropriate salary schedules.

While this is an excellent model which, we would assume, is followed for
existing job classifications and by larger governmental jurisdictions, the evidence
suggests state government typically is less flexible, less appropriate in relating
entry requirements with type and level of training, and less inclined to provide
salary scales which recognize the middle manpower level.

Florida provides an illustration. The state of Florida has established 22 area
vocational-technical centers and a system of 28 operating community colleges in
an effort to meet the middle manpower demand of the 1970's.

The fiscal year ending June 30, 1970, saw over 20,000 completions from area
vocational-technical centers and community colleges in two-year occupational
programs. On the basis of pilot follow-up studies, it has been estimated that only
one-half of the graduates were employed full-time in the field for which they
trained.

Approximately one-third chose to continue their education, get married, enter
the military or otherwise voluntarily go another direction. The remainder, it is
assumed, were unable to enter the middle manpower field which they had chosen. Utilization therefore was less than ideal as we identify potential opportunities in industry or government.

During this same period, a review of the state government class specifications
for all jobs within the Florida Career Service revealed little or no recognition of
the two-year occupational education graduate. There were more than 70,000
positions within the Florida Career Service. Yet, the class specifications included
only 18 classes which recognized vocational-technical school or community college occupational education as proper training (three-fourths of which are in the
allied health field).

Equally discouraging was the fact many of the classes recognized general academic education of baccalaureate level as substituting for any part of the required occupational experience. Less than 8% of the classes reflected middle
manpower training recognition, although it was estimated that as many as 60%
of all occupational jobs fell in the middle manpower range requiring some type
of postsecondary occupational education.

Most states are no better off than Florida in providing for clear entry levels for
middle manpower graduates. General catch-all classifications have been created
in Pennsylvania and New York, but correlation of task requirements with training programs has not been provided.

California is credited with the best record of relating local governmental agency job requirements with the specific program offerings of local postsecondary
institutions. Its state service classifications cannot make the same claim, however.

Florida has undertaken a project intended to close its middle manpower utilization gap. The Florida State University, under a grant from the Division of Vocational, Technical and Adult Education, Florida State Department of Education, initiated a study in 1971 based on the general hypothesis that rungs were missing in the career ladder at the middle manpower level. Five purposes were identified:

1. To develop greater societal understanding and acceptance of occupational preparation at the technical, semi-professional, and mid-management levels offered by postsecondary occupational education programs with particular emphasis, initially, upon the two-year program level at area vocational-technical centers and community colleges.
2. To provide new entry levels in government, industry, and business based on skills, competencies, and knowledge gained in postsecondary occupational education programs, but eventually to include all types of formal postsecondary training regardless of duration.
3. To provide the model and rationale for meaningful career-ladder opportunities through differentiated staffing.
4. To foster clearly identifiable compensation schedules for occupational education graduates with initial emphasis upon the two-year postsecondary program graduates.
5. To contribute to cost effectiveness and accountability in personnel utilization by avoiding the practice of under employment of highly trained people.

Phase I of the project was a planning study to determine the feasibility of accomplishing the stated purposes. This was done through a literature search, through consultation with national authorities, and through a series of conferences with those state agencies which would be involved in the future implementation of the project.

Cultural Lag

It was necessary to create the climate whereby the agency officials could internalize the value and desirability of the project, for they could be included in Heinz Eulau's observation that "Political behavior patterns and institutions are particularly subject to cultural lag because they are sanctified by customs and traditions." A plan for implementation evolved from Phase I.

Project CTMMUG (Closing the Middle Manpower Utilization Gap) was initiated in 1972 as a pilot study using the Department of Transportation as the target agency. The objectives of the project were:

1. To examine job classes used by the department of transportation and make recommendations for those classes identified as appropriate for revision.

2. To undertake a general task analysis of each class to determine the skill, competency, and knowledge requirements of each.
3. To identify area center or community college programs which relate to competencies required for specific classes under review.
4. To identify recruiting efforts, statewide, directed toward middle manpower utilization.
5. To foster an interface between the user (department of transportation) and the producers (educational institutions) to gain needed changes by both.
6. To give visibility to the outcomes of the project in order that other agencies might follow the example made.

Great Potential

By the end of 1972 it was apparent that Project CTMMUG had great potential if broadened to other agencies and if the concept were applied regionally and nationally. Approximately 10% of the 336 job classes in the DOT were found to be appropriate for graduates of community college occupational programs. Recommendations were made covering 1806 job positions statewide. The success of the pilot study led to a renewal of funding for the present year.

Community colleges and their state-level agencies throughout the nation should consider an examination of governmental entry requirements in their own state. This would hasten closing the utilization gap and provide more job opportunities for occupational education graduates.

The same concept and need applies to business and industrial firms as well. As our instructional programs are increasingly designed on competency-based objectives, it is imperative that we work closely with the employers to assure appropriate training and instruction. But the employers must play a more dominant role in identifying and providing commensurate compensation scales for middle manpower entry levels. While many years may be needed before the goal will be achieved, every effort to bring public understanding and employer commitment is one more step toward placing the missing rung in the career ladder.

PART 5

Career Education in Perspective

Meeting Our Enemies, Career Education
and the Humanities
by Sidney P. Marland, Jr.

Career Education: Theory and Practice
by Margueritte and Robert Caldwell

Expanding on Career Education
by Raymond E. Wanner

In a nation that has perpetual unemployment, welfare recipients, and school drop-outs; that finds significant numbers of young people involved in projects and works not for monetary gain but for the possible opportunities to effect positive changes in their society; and in a nation that has exploited the nineteenth century work ethic concept so that the dignity of labor does not carry the old connotations, the advocacy of Career Education as a means to return to possibly outmoded principles would seem to be fraught with possible dire consequences. Career Education programs must include a review of the work ethic concept in terms of its applications to today's society and the society of the future.

Clifton Fadiman, in Occasional Paper Number Twenty of the Council for Basic Education entitled *What Is Career Education?* asks Marland some penetrating questions and suggests that "the unconscious drive of some advocates of Career Education . . . is to condition the technological serf who will be with us during the next two or three hundred years . . ." and he further suggests that our new technologies are beginning to outmode the classic work ethic. If Career Education is supported in the belief that it will help to maintain the *status quo* by perpetuating the work ethic, these supporters may become disappointed, or perhaps more dangerous, because they may be able to convert the aims of Career Education and defeat the students, the society, and themselves.

Not only is Career Education in danger because it may be supported for inappropriate reasons, it also must gain the understanding, acceptance and support of the taxpayers, the academicians, the parents, the students, the employers, and the teachers—in effect the support of the total community.

Teachers often appear loathe to accept change for a variety of reasons both real and imaginary. Schools are supposed (by many) to support the *status quo* and teachers have seen educational "fads" come and go as they remained secure in their tenured positions.

Academicians, as the Caldwells indicate, have reservations about Career Education and a realistic definition of the work ethic. Employers relying on past performance may not have the greatest faith in the school system's ability to deliver trained entry-level personnel. Unions may interpret Career Education as a threat to their autonomy.

The success of Career Education will rest in the acceptance of the program's concepts by the students and the parents whose lives are most directly affected by Career Education. The final assessment and the ultimate development of Career Education is up to you. This volume is designed as a guide to Career Education. It offers insights into specific aspects of Career Education as they relate to school and society, and as they relate to change and future shock.

Sidney P. Marland

MEETING OUR ENEMIES, CAREER EDUCATION AND THE HUMANITIES*

Career education and the humanities is a topic that reminds me of a comment by one of our lesser known Presidents, Franklin Pierce (1853 to 1857), reinforced by a better known personality, Pogo. While Pierce may not flash to mind when drawing up a list of Great Americans, Pogo may well qualify.

Pierce is quoted from 1855, two years after he assumed the Presidency. The occasion was an off-year election, in which Mr. Pierce's followers hopefully submitted themselves to the verdict of the voters—and were thoroughly trounced. Reading the dismaying returns, Mr. Pierce commented: "We have met the enemy—and we are theirs." Pogo's well-known paraphrase, you will recall, is, "We have met the enemy and they are us." (I cannot help wishing that he had had greater respect for an intransitive verb and the predicate nominative. But I am afraid "They are we" just isn't Pogo.)

Humanists—among whom, as an English teacher, I number myself—have done much the same. We have met the enemy, and we are theirs—or, possibly, they are we. In any event, for decades we have allowed ourselves to be steadily trounced by those who regard our discipline as a genteel but fundamentally trivial concern with sweetness, light, and iambic pentameter, and unrelated to the utilitarian world.

Maybe, there is more truth than fiction in this accusation. Certainly many humanists are disquieted by the notion of career education and concerned about its potential effect on curriculum. But to justify our endeavor, I think we *must* establish a close tie between career education and the humanities because, as an instructional strategy, career education is aimed at improving educational outcomes by relating *all* teaching and learning activities to the concept of career development.

This statement may confirm the worst fears of those among us who look askance at career education. If I had to guess at those fears, I would say they run something like this: "Career education is the mad culmination of the 'relevance' kick of recent years. It is a rejection by the Federal Government of the liberal,

*S. P. Marland, Jr.—"Meeting Our Enemies, Career Education and the Humanities" reprinted by permission of the publisher and the author from the September, 1973 issue of the *English Journal* copyright © 1973 by the National Council of Teachers of English.

humanistic tradition in education in favor of a strictly pragmatic, utilitarian approach focused entirely on employment and income. Career education is a euphemism for mechanistic job-training, and it is fundamentally anti-intellectual."

I'm overstating, perhaps, but I nonetheless suspect that those remarks come pretty close to expressing sentiments of some academic teachers in the high schools and colleges of America. As you would expect, I disavow each of them—for reasons that I hope you will find convincing by the time I finish. But because abstract argument is so rarely convincing, let me go at this discussion by examining, first, the specific substance of career education.

We conceive of career education as beginning in kindergarten or first grade. Until the sixth grade, there would be no attempt to *train* students. All we are aiming at in these early years is developing an awareness of careers, a personal realization that each student will spend most of his or her life doing or being something—and that "something" will be largely determined by work. *Work* may or may not carry economic motivations—but it is seen as the product of useful living. Also, we want to give the young a sense of the remarkable number of options that will be open to them, to inform them of the manifold ways by which adults in this society go about the business of living productively.

The latest Department of Labor *Dictionary of Occupational Titles* lists about 23,000 different occupations. Obviously we cannot hope to teach youngsters much about so great a number. However, we can group the great majority of those titles into clusters of related occupations. A hospital orderly; a medical technician, a nurse, and a brain-surgeon, for example, are all related, so we refer to these as being in the "health cluster."

We have identified fifteen such clusters. The others are agri-business and natural resources; business and office; communication and media; consumer and homemaking; construction; environment; fine arts and humanities; hospitality and recreation; manufacturing; marine science; marketing and distribution; personal services; public service; and transportation. It's worth noting, for this audience, that the "fine arts and humanities" cluster includes poet, novelist, and painter. We are not trying to turn everybody into a machinist.

Clusters reduce the 23,000 occupational possibilities to a manageable number so that we can develop curricular materials around them. Inasmuch as most of the curricular effort at this point is being directed at the secondary level, however, most of the classroom activity for elementary-level career education must come from the initiative and imagination of individual teachers—and some interesting things have been happening all around the country under our model development system.

A fourth-grade teacher in one Michigan community, for example, invited an industrial physicist from a nearby Pontiac facility to talk to her youngsters. His talk related conveniently to some of the concepts the class had been discussing in science. But in language arts, the youngsters had been discussing interviewing techniques, and after the physicist put his equipment away, he was grilled by the class: How long did he have to study for his job? Did he have to go to college? Was it important for a physicist to like science and math as a child? Did he get good grades in those subjects when he was in school? How much money did he make?

It was, in sum, a genuine interview, motivated by honest curiosity. They were *real* questions, asked by youngsters who wanted to *know* something. During the year, ninety adults from different occupations—the mayor, an electrician, an insurance salesman, a beautician—visited that one school, opening for those youngsters a window on the world in a real way that no amount of lecturing or reading could have accomplished. In our present culture it is very difficult for a child to walk beside his father at the plow and learn about work. We are trying to find substitutes.

In seventh and eighth grade, youngsters move beyond this broad occupational awareness phase. By this time, they know something about all the clusters, and have begun to relate them to their own interests. They have learned quite a bit, too, about their own aptitudes—which subjects they're good in, which ones they're so-so in, which ones they find the most fun.

They know enough about themselves and about careers, in short, to make a reasonably solid judgement about which of the fifteen clusters appeal to them most, and to choose a few—we think three is a good number—for more systematic exploration. And in ninth grade, after two years of this narrowing exploration, they will know enough about the three occupational clusters they've been studying to make a tentative selection of one as their field for further and more concentrated career preparation. It is important to underscore *tentative*, since career education calls for open options at all levels of learning.

It is at this point (at about age 13–14) that something undeniably and unblushingly recognizable as job-training begins. Our goal is that during the last four years of schooling—the ninth through twelfth grades—every youngster will develop entry-level job skills that will qualify him for employment upon leaving school, *whenever* he leaves.

I repeat, *every* youngster—including those who intend to go on to college or some other form of postsecondary education. If, by tenth grade, a girl has decided that she wants to take a Ph.D. in molecular biology, fine; not only are we for her, but we stand in awe of her knowledge of what the words mean. Recognizing the uncertain nature of life and the changeability of young minds and spirits, however, we want to give her a fall-back position if her plans don't work out—to make sure that she can qualify for a good job even if she leaves high school *before* graduation. Moreover, even if that job won't be at the level to which she originally aspired, at least she will have adequate skills in an occupational area that interests her—in this case, the health cluster. Finally, if her circumstances *do* improve, she retains the option and the qualification to return for higher academic training—at any time—perhaps years later.

This is a major point to be made about each of the occupational clusters: each includes a range of employment opportunities that can accommodate every type of aptitude, every level of intellect. The construction cluster, for instance, has room for young men who prefer outdoor manual labor—and, these days, for young women who prefer outdoor, manual labor. This cluster also has room for entrepreneurs who aspire to operate their own contracting business someday. It has room for engineers concerned with the strength of materials, and for architects concerned with beauty and function. And it has room for new specialties emerging in economic fields such as environmental science, urban planning, and new town management.

In our thinking about occupations and careers, then, we have been careful to make room for the hands and the hammer and the honest skill it takes to drive a nail straight. But we give equal voice to the imagination and the spirit, for the man who cannot fix a faucet but can dream a new concept of community. These are all parts of one whole, each with its own dignity and importance, and we make no apology for teaching the future architect what a carpenter does or teaching the future carpenter the liberalizing joys of Robert Browning and Edna St. Vincent Millay. It is well past time for our educational institutions to help eliminate prejudice based on work—to overcome the idea, passed on to us by our own parents, that some jobs are worthy and some are not, that some family heads are to be respected and others are scorned, and that the best way to tell the difference is to see whether the wage earner owns a college degree or wears a tie to work.

By twelfth grade, then, our plan is that career education will have prepared every youngster for an entry-level job in the occupational cluster of his choice. We remind ourselves that we will have about 22 percent of our young dropping out before high school graduation. If career education does not entice them to stay, at least we believe it will qualify them for something better than the streets.

But career education is not merely job-getting. Nor is it a competitor or adversary to the high traditions of academic teaching and learning. The academic skills are still the school's principal *raison d' etre*. But we believe young people in school and college will learn them better, with more ease and interest, because their mathematics, language arts, sciences, and social studies have been related to purposes which students perceive as important to their own future lives. Career education is not a substitute for the old curriculum, even though it entails the use of some new materials; rather, it is a new *context* for learning, a new way of viewing curriculum. Every teacher knows that the single, most powerful teaching force in a classroom is motivating students. We believe that career education will do that, at any level the student finds personally significant. All good teachers have intuitively and sensitively tried to relate learning to life. Career education moves us along this road, systematically, hopefully with richer materials and a better knowledge on the part of the learner as to why he is learning.

The result will be better preparation for whatever path the student chooses to follow after leaving high school, or after high school graduation. He can get a job. He can enter a technical institute for more intensive, specialized preparation for a career. Or he can enter a four-year college—and with a much better sense of direction than most young adults bring to college today.

This has been a once-over-lightly treatment of career education as it is unfolding today as a high priority in the Office of Education.

One could go on at length, scolding ourselves over the failure of the schools to equip approximately half of our newly enfranchised 18-year-olds for college *or* for a job. I will not labor it. Suffice it to say here that the Office of Education is not under any delusion concerning the need for reform and the complexities of the task.

We know that relating academic teaching to the career theme cannot be accomplished in a bureau in Washington. Hence, we have established fifteen advisory groups made up of teachers and practitioners in each of the occupational clusters to help us relate job requirements to basic academic skills. We have contracted with some of the nation's leading curriculum specialists to develop high school curricula for five of the fifteen clusters so far—construction, manufacturing, transportation, public service, and communications and media. Several should be ready for pilot-testing next year. We expect to fund development of two more cluster curriculums, probably sales and office occupations, shortly.

We have not undertaken lightly a reform of this impressive scope. Learning from educational experiments of the past, we do not believe that a few snappy slogans and some Federal money can accomplish any serious educational reform—and we are very candidly talking about reform. We have a staggering amount of thinking, experimentation, and refining to do, and probably a distressing number of mistakes still to make.

But at this point I want to depart from explaining what career education is in itself to talk about its relation to the humanities, because I think that educators interested in the humanities—the liberal arts—also have some thinking to do, and some work to do, if the career education proposition is found worthy of their interest and ultimately successful in their classrooms.

Career education, to begin with, need not spell the "Death of Intellect in the West." Even should it find universal acceptance, it will still be possible for a student to pursue truth and beauty, not to mention syntax and composition, without first investigating how much it pays per hour. But out of sincere respect for all who entertain misgivings, I want to turn to a necessarily brief discussion of what may be the continuing evolution of the liberal tradition in education.

Most Americans, I believe, think of formal academic education as a privilege that was once restricted to the elite in society, but gradually—after great struggle and the passage of centuries—became accessible to the less-favored masses, to virtually everyone, in fact, who seeks it in our country. This hypothesis leads to a hasty assumption in the light of general human experience, which is that nice things are found first by the favored.

But with education, it is not true. Education in western Europe, and notably in England, did *not* start at the top. It started in the middle. During most of the Middle Ages, both serfs *and* the nobles were illiterate. It was only the ambitious sons of the embryonic middle class who saw education as their avenue to up-ward-mobility. (Parenthetically, this phenomenon is now dominant in America, as we seek upward mobility for our own least favored.) Returning to the Middle Ages, there were two acceptable opportunities through schooling: a career in the church or a career as a merchant. For such careers literacy was an absolute essential. As late as the 18th century, some members of the House of Lords were still illiterate. If you find this difficult to believe, open your Henry Fielding, study Squire Western, and ask yourself if Oxford or Cambridge would claim him as an alumnus. For a more recent reference, open your Evelyn Waugh, study Sir Alastair Trumpington of *Decline and Fall*, and ask yourself if his presence at Scone College had any discernible relation to education.

It was not until the Renaissance, with the rediscovrry of ancient Greek and Roman literature and language, that learning became fashionable for the upper classes. From this era, in fact, we can date the beginning of humanisim in western Europe. For the first time, men could read something about themselves as men, could consider the human experience as something important in itself rather than as a reflection of the omnipotence of God, and significant therefore only in relation to afterlife and the certainties of death, judgement, heaven, or hell. And it was only after the Renaissance that the sons of wealthy men began entering the universities, competing with and often crowding out less affluent scholars. Chaucer gives us a picture of university students in the early 13th century; they were all broke.

The point is that formal education in the West started with a distinctly occu-pational orientation. It was *not* learning for its own sake. It was learning for a specific career purpose such as demanded by the market place, the church, the money lender, the healer. But with the entrance of the rich into higher edu-cation came a gradual isolation of learning from work. Rich young men, after all, would not *have* to work. For the, cultivation of intellect became desirable in itself, apart from any use to which a trained mind might be put.

The influx of affluent students, their freedom from the necessity of vocational preparation, the prestige of their superior status, and the secular subjects then available for study shaped the form and substance of classical education, in-cluding a gradual cleavage between liberal and utilitarian studies. Thus, some very eloquent spokesmen for the liberal tradition received a distinctly vocational education without recognizing it. John Henry Newman, for example, whose *Idea of a University* remains a classic of literature as well as of educational theory, studied Greek, Latin, Hebrew, and the Church Fathers. This is as distinctly *un*-vocational an education as one can imagine—unless one is studying to be, as Newman became, an ecclesiastical scholar of heroic proportions.

It seems to me that many of us who care about the humanities and work in them daily are laboring under an intellectual misconception about where we came from. Anxious sustainers of the truth, we man the battlements of our ancient castle, ready to defend it against the onslaught of science and auto mechanics and data-processing and other heathen disciplines as though they were the other side, rather than our companions. Believing that nobody over twenty-one will pay any attention, we vainly and self-destrictively repeat unexamined formulas: "The liberal arts do not teach one how to make a living," we say, "they teach one how to live." What awful nonsense. While English teachers can rightly account for the infinite array of human need to which we bend our profession, the humanities in general need our support in the larger sense.

It is high time for us to examine more closely what we refer to as our "tradition in the humanities," and ask ourselves whether we are passing it on alive and young, rejuvenated by our own fresh interpretation of the meaning of the humanities for a changing world, or whether we are simply handing on an old package that sombody else told us was valuable. Knowledge is *not* its own end. It it were, there would be no qualitative difference between reading Toynbee and reading the World Almanac. Both convey knowledge, but the manner of the conveyance is the difference between a towering intellectual performance that lifts the spirit and commands admiration, and a compendium of facts that occasionally comes in handy. None of us reads poetry for the sake of reading a poem. We read good poetry for intellectual and aesthetic pleasure—and intangible as these pleasures are, they are just as *real* as the pleasures that come from enjoying a good meal, playing a good game of tennis, or getting a good contract signed on the dotted line. These various forms of pleasure satisfy human appetites, and even though we properly distinguish among these appetites and may rank some above others, they nevertheless crave satisfaction in all of us.

What has this homily to do with career education?

There is a saying from the Talmud that goes like this: "When you stop working, you're dead." As I interpret it, this does not mean that the foreman will shoot if you lay down your shovel, or the superintendent will frown if your daily planning book is awry. It means, rather, that when you stop working at your*self*, when you regard yourself as a finished piece of goods with no prospect of growth or surprise or becoming, then you are indeed, as the advertisement says, "dead at 30, retired at 65." Work, in other words, has a *central position in the fashioning of a satisfactory human life,* and I hold this to be true especially for those who dare to teach the young! We do not teach for money, nor for status, nor for some fatuous prominence, but for facilitating human happiness. And if the humanities have nothing to say to students about a matter so crucial to their future contentment and fulfillment as work, then I must ask whether humanists have not become futile curators of a world that vanished years ago, when the nobility discovered Latin.

If universal affluence ever breaks out, and the problems of poverty, blessedly go away, we won't have to look far for other problems to solve: boredom, for example, is staring us in the face, and boredom—as any psychiatrist, clergyman, or marriage counselor can tell you—is a serious, pervasive human problem. Its remedies rest in the resources possessed by English teachers, music teachers, physical education teachers, art teachers, history teachers, social scientists.

Humanists must lend a hand in reinterpreting for our society the vital significance of work for man and its place in any modern conception of education. There *are* important, worthwhile distinctions to be made between liberal and utilitarian studies—but we humanists have not been making them. Instead we have acquiesced in a cynical perspective that views work as something we put up with between nine and five so we can do what interests us after the plant closes down. At its worst, work is a dreary, painful chore. At its best in our society—a society that can name 23,000 different jobs—work is an opportunity for self-exploration; at its best, work *is* a humanity—and we have the chance to help our youngsters approach work as their intellectual and personal fulfillment. If teaching is not that, then what is it?

Career education aims at fulfilling some undeniably pragmetic goals, partially definable in terms of Gross National Product, taxes paid, employment increased, and welfare payments no longer needed. But it also probes some deeply human concerns, and if the humanities can stand passively by while so many human beings hurt—while so many human beings know *how* to, but have forgotten *why* to—then I must ask what the humanities are for.

We need humanists to help us elaborate and refine this concept of career education. We need humanists to guide our groping for these deeper human concerns on the job and off the job. And it may be that *we humanists ourselves need such a highly utilitarian exercise* to sweep us back into youth and remind us of our original purpose—which is to buttress the spirit with the knowledge that another man, in another time, passed this way before, suffered and joyed as we do, and paid his dues for the magnificent privilege and heavy responsibility of being human, especially in this remarkable land of ours. Neither centuries nor social station can separate us; only our own intellectual myopia can.

Look around. Our beleaguered castle is not really being assaulted by the champions of other disciplines called occupational. They're not attacking our fortress at all. They're just detouring around it, because so many of them, including students, don't think we guard anything worth taking. If we in the humanities continue to regard more "practical" people as our enemies, and if we continue to be theirs—it will be our own damn fault.

Marguerite and Robert Caldwell

CAREER EDUCATION: THEORY AND PRACTICE*

In his 1971 paper on career education, Sidney Marland argued that students should become more familiar with the world of work before they enter it. Few English teachers would quarrel with that assertion, for nowhere else, perhaps, does a wider gap exist between expectation and fulfillment than in the teacher's own profession: In theory it is an academic and demanding discipline requiring training, dedication, and skill for its proper execution, but in practice the plumber and the clerk elected to the local board of education and speaking for the community at large exert an authority in curricular affairs out of all proportion to their competence. A discrepency between theory and practice begins in the college classroom itself, where the embryonic teacher often learns his profession from a group of people who frequently have had little first-hand experience in high school teaching themselves, but who are nevertheless confident about what should be taught in the schools. We are all familiar with theories of education that work well enough in a vacuum, perhaps, but in the modern high school English class (where they are supposed to apply) they are often ludicrously inappropriate. Given the kind of understanding of the realities of the workaday world that Marland speaks of, perhaps a good many English teachers might well have chosen different careers.

Other areas of agreement are more difficult to come by, for the career education movement seems to share the presumption that people currently *outside* the teaching profession are more qualified to offer direction and set its policy than those *within*. The implications of external control in this instance are obviously very serious, because the concentrated resources of the U.S. Office of Education have been committed "to effect a thorough and permanent improvement" in American schools. Unless this improvement is genuine, the districts and states that adopt such programs will be damaged considerably. Thus it is important to be as clear as possible in discussing career education and to separate what its proponents *say* from what they seem to *mean*.

Career education is partly a revolt against alleged weaknesses of general education, partly a theory about human nature, and partly a defense of American technology. Marland's greatest concern is what he sees as the schools' failure to

---

*Margueritte and Robert Caldwell—"Career Education: Theory and Practice" reprinted by permission of the publisher and the author from the September, 1973 issue of the *English Journal* copyright © 1973 by the National Council of Teachers of English.

171

meet the career requirements of thousands of discontented students, including the failure to satisfy the "career demands of the astonishingly complex technological society that we live in" and the failure to contribute to the students' personal fulfillment as human beings. Career education is intended to rectify these ills, not only by giving every student a marketable skill by the time he graduates from high school, but by refocussing classes in the basic subject areas in such a way that all of them contribute directly and exclusively to this end. Anything else, we are told, amounts to "irrelevant, general educational pap."

By getting rid of general education, Marland also hopes to eliminate certain other ills that plague both the schools and the society at large. When classes become more meaningful to students, i.e., more relevant to their needs as potential job holders in business and industry, the perennial problem of student motivation will no longer exist. These classes, appropriately restructured, will then be recognized as necessary for the realization of the student's own creative potential. With everyone properly programmed to perform an eventual and essential role in America's technological society, student dropouts will be minimized, the current widespread ignorance of one's own interests and attitudes will be eliminated, general disenchantment with the world of work will turn to admiration, and excessive welfare payments in the country at large will no longer be necessary.

This relatively straightforward account of career education has been complicated, however, by a number of citizens who apparently feel that any radical change in educational policy is bound to sacrifice something of value. Thus in a publication entitled *Career Education: A Handbook for Implementation,* the Maryland State Board of Education tells us that career education is defined in many ways but that it doesn't conflict with other "legitimate education objectives such as citizenship, culture, family responsibility, and basic education." And we are told in an Arizona State Department of Education pamphlet called "Career Education Matrix" that career education is an approach to learning which represents expanded options for young people. Perhaps so. But if Marland's account is accurate, what it actually offers is expanded *career* options at the cost of some others that have nothing directly to do with the world of work but much to do with the right conduct of our lives. The Arizona pamphlet goes on to say that career education attempts "to develop schools as a gateway to personal future (sic) through the development of values and the gaining of wisdom." And while this statement also seems to be in conflict with Marland's stress on the world of work where wisdom has at best a functionary role, it turns out to be either a cynical attempt to convince the orthodox teacher that career education is really not the radical proposal that it seems to be, or else it implies a half-formed conviction that career education need not be quite as career oriented as Marland suggests.

Vague as it is, however, even this conviction seems inconsistent with statements made by those interested in career education. For if we ask *what* values and *what* wisdom are important, we find another pamphlet widely used in

Arizona by career counselors, that simply begs the question. "Values," we are solemnly assured, "can only be judged by the individual for himself." But judged how? In terms of the decision maker's own personal preferences so that what he prefers cannot be wrong as long as he prefers it? Then the only sort of development of values that is possible is a change from one to another, not because the first is discovered to *have* no value but simply because one grows tired of it and wants a change. How much wisdom is found in this way of understanding the language of values we leave to the discerning reader to decide. But any teacher of literature who believes that all values are on a par with one another and that no real justification can ever be given for preferring temperance to lechery or honesty to fraud has already lost the battle. Given this point of view on the nature and worth of values, it is no wonder that traditional education is sometimes regarded as incompetent, irrelevant, and immaterial by its critics.

However this issue of values is to be resolved, it is clear that we have a number of incompatible accounts of what career education is (and these accounts can easily be multiplied), and the wonder is, therefore, that so many people are convinced of its supposed benefits and so much energy is expended in trying to implement it. Surely the traditional school curriculum is not in such a cancerous state that even ambiguous or incoherent alternatives are preferable to it, especially in view of the fact that little evidence is offered in support of the thesis that schools are the cause of the evils found therein.

Doubtless the schools provide the context in which certain unfortunate events occur, but to assume these contexts are also the *causes* of the events is to beg the question at issue. Students can drop out of school only if they attend it, of course, as they can fall out of airplanes only if they fly, but in neither case do the circumstances in which these occurrences take place also function inevitably as their causes. Thus, although it is true that some students do not complete school, do not select careers wisely, and do not have more than a superficial knowledge of themselves, the cause of these events is still an open question; and unless self-awareness is defined as an increased understanding of one's attitudes and interests *vis-a-vis* the world of work rather than something more nearly akin to Socratic self-knowledge, the schools are clearly not the cause of the existing self-ignorance but its cure.

This failure to justify some of the claims made about career education is in fact one of its most serious theoretical weaknesses, though in view of the nature of the claims being made, perhaps this failure is understandable. Why is it our dual responsibility, for example, "to meet the student's needs on the one hand and to satisfy the country's infinite social and economic appetites on the other?" Doubtless no one would question the first of these duties unless student needs are defined in a way that we cannot accept, but considerable objection could be made to the second. Are we to satisfy any economic appetite, for instance, no matter how trivial, wasteful, or demeaning it might be, and more significantly, are we to train students to classify this sort of question as irrelevant educational pap because it is not part of the curriculum whose aim is to do precisely what we are here challenging? Surely the proper response to infinite economic appetites in a world of finite natural resources is not unlimited self-indulgence but rational self-control, a notion, incidentally, that the career specialist in his professional capacity is hardly prepared to judge. When we consider how student needs are to be understood in this context, moreover, are we not warranted in raising some objections to our so-called responsibility of trying to satisfy them? Apparently a need is defined here as anything that contributes to a successful career in business or industry and thus as anything that equips a person "to live his life as a fulfilled human being." But of course human needs are not merely economic in nature, and a human being is not just a two-dimensional cut-out whose notions of success and self-fulfillment rest solely on financial considerations. Perhaps mankind *is* becoming closer and closer to this economic "ideal," but if so we hope education plays no part in fostering it.

This litany of criticism could be continued at some length. In an article entitled "On The Job," for instance, *Focus Magazine* reports that students are not questioning the relevance of school as much as they are challenging the work ethic itself. And in *Newsweek* we find that the world of work faces many of the same difficulties that confront the schools. Workers in the automotive industry are notoriously dissatisfied with their jobs, for example, as their production frequently shows, and this dissatisfaction is serious and widespread enough in other industries to convince even the Nixon Administration to spend $2 million this year to study it. Surely, then, the alienation of the worker cannot be due chiefly to the schools that fail to identify student attitudes and interests properly or to point the way to a more self-fulfilling career.

We see no reason to believe, in short, that career education is a cure for the ills that threaten contemporary American schools, that the self-fulfillment offered by career education is identical to human fulfillment (though doubtless it is part of it), that career education educates the whole man along with that part of him concerned with making a living, and that meeting the career demands of American technology is synonymous with meeting the real needs of the country. The attempt to modify the structure of American education, therefore, to conform to an ideal that is not only incompletely and inconsistently worked out but faulty in conception as well seems to us to be a mistake.

For all its inconsistencies and misconceptions, however, we are convinced that career education is here to stay. Its slogans, concepts, and rationale, as difficult as they are to put together logically, still appeal to parents, employers, and the public at large, because they focus on earning power, security, and measurable objectives at a time when the schools are coming more and more under attack. The promise of federal and state aid, moreover, exerts a powerful influence on the thinking of local taxpayers, many of whom are relatively indifferent to what goes on in the schools as long as it doesn't cost them money. If the federal government is willing to accept the financial burden, they seem to suggest, then why not let them build the freeways in our cities and set the curriculum for our schools?

But if this is the conviction we are left with, what should we do about it? Simply acquiese to the career educationalists? Pretend to comply with them for the obvious financial returns? Or can we effect a compromise (without abdicating any of our responsibilities to our students) by showing career educationalists how much the concerned and competent English teacher is doing to prepare the student to cope with the world, including the world of work, and then hope that the resources of the U.S. Office of Education will be used to further these legitimate goals and not to thwart them? Only the last of these alternatives seems to us to be worthy of serious consideration and this is the one we intend to explain and defend.

To take these alternatives in order, we cannot simply acquiese to the career education movement because then the child would have to explore the work ethic concept from the time he enters kindergarten until he either becomes a dropout or is graduated. Acquiescence would mean that the child on the primary levels would not only have to recognize "that his career includes progression through developmental stages of educational and occupational experiences," but he would also have to "understand the variety of occupations found in the world of work and would need to learn how occupations relate to the needs and functions of society." So much for ages five, six, and seven.

Some people in career education would argue that we are misreading their position and show us a color-coded flow chart that has the appealing slogan, "Learning to Live, Learning to Learn, Learning to Make a Living." At first reading, the slogan is reassuring because it includes not only the workaday world but also those other worlds that today's students have demonstrated they need so desperately. But a closer examination of the matrix developing this slogan indicates a much narrower scope. The "elements of career education" and their matching "outcomes" make very explicit the direction all English classes should take. Words like "careers," "job opportunities," and "work ethic" have such a high frequency that "Learning to Make a Living" dominates throughout.

To make the point more explicit, the eight elements of career education according to this flow chart are self-awareness, education awareness, career awareness, economic awareness, decision making, beginning competence, employability skills, and appreciations and attitudes. The range again seems to include the whole student; and what English teacher with the best interests of his students at heart could object to any of them? Indeed, what English teacher's files do not include lesson plans on the theme "Who am I," on persuasive language, decision making, and on "I'm O.K.; you're O.K."?

But in the long lists of sub-goals on this particular flow chart, the main stress is again on utilitarian values. Of the eight elements listed, four are heavily job-oriented for all grades K–12. Of the forty-three goals listed under "self-awareness," ten singularly stress work. Of the twenty-five goals to develop appreciation and attitudes, sixteen center on job preparation. Even in an area which promises to further the affective domain, the emphasis on career requirements is strong.

On the other hand, of the forty-five goals listed under career awareness, all forty-five focus on careers. In brief, out of 113 goals ascribed to the three elements of this matrix, more than half require that the students explore the world of work. Put it another way, even if we want to develop units on self-awareness or appreciation, we must keep in mind that our primary goal is to define the students as wage earners, not as human beings.

Thus even when proponents of career education claim that their proposals do not conflict with other legitimate educational goals such as the exploration of human relationships, civic responsibility, and personal fulfillment, we cannot acquiesce to them because these subordinate goals often tend to be mutilated or ignored in the crush of everyday school experiences.

The second alternative—"riding along" with the movement—is equally unworthy of serious consideration because it involves us in deliberate or accidental deception without commitment. Teachers may accept the largess of career education knowing full well that they are not going beyond the courtship stage with it, or they may naively misconstrue incidental or superficial similarities with identity. A teacher in the first category justifies his actions by pointing to the results. The department benefits by getting tape recorders, field trips, and lots of relevant resource material for the classroom. Once obtained, the material can be used in any way the department wishes. As one teacher remarked, "I can always find some connection between what career education wants and what I am doing in the classroom, no matter how tenuous. A career education program bought us Ninety copies of _____ because it talks about houses of the future. We got a nice field trip out of them, too. The kids got to see new kinds of architecture; we showed them a university campus which most had never seen."

A more absurd example of teacher myopia is the teacher of English who is studying *Richard III* with a group of multi-ethnic students. He is having his students list all the occupations mentioned in the play because career education specialists have said this is one way of integrating the two disciplines. (A facetious alternative suggested to him is Golding's *Lord of the Flies* where job clusters abound: construction, military, foods and services, and law enforcement. And to cap it off, the novel would provide a realistic, graphic example of the axiom, "If you don't work, you don't eat.")

The third approach toward meeting the challenge of career education is a compromise in which the concerned and competent English teacher helps to prepare students to cope with both the world of language and the world of work. The best English teachers—those with intelligence, superior training, knowledge of social problems, sensitivities for students' needs, and sensibilities in meeting them—*do* incorporate many of the goals that career education proposes. With an eye on the needs and nature of students, we have related our discipline to the real world. Admittedly we have not directed the student solely toward learning about the world of work or searching for a specific job, but we have good reasons for neglecting to do so. We feel such action would harm students at a time when specific jobs are becoming obsolete almost daily, when the Asimovs and the Tofflers predict that a person may well be re-trained three or four times to meet job requirements in the age of technocracy.

We have avoided dominating the students' thirteen years of schooling with information about job opportunities and an exploration of society's attitude toward the work ethnic because we see students as complete human beings, not as workers or technicians. We have concentrated on the affective processes as well as the cognitive and psychomotor to the neglect of none. Through our guidance students have improved their reasoning skills and have learned through doing. They have explored who they are and what they might become. They have had time to dream their dreams.

We English teachers have not shut ourselves in a castle of medievalism while students detour around us. We counsel them, we study them, we scold and praise. We work with them and for them, convinced that our discipline is in the mainstream of their lives. Our methods have the style of this time; our constantly re-examined goals, the shape of this age.

What English teacher, good or bad, has not taught letter writing, the report, applying for a job, interviewing, punctuation, usage, effective choice of words, spelling, critical reading of newspapers, the language of ads, mass media persuasive techniques, writing telegrams, identifying fallacies, panel participation, the range of information in a telephone directory, writing to senior citizens as foster grandparents, applying to university admission offices, and slide tapes for expressing ideas?

What teacher's room has not held bulletin boards showing today's youth meeting today's problems through some aspect of English? What English department does not have current magazines, newspapers, films, film strips and AV equipment as signs of that real world? Which ones do not have course descriptions of the practical: Consumer English, Business English, Happenings in Language, Vocabulary Power, How to Win an Argument, Basic Conposition, Vocations and Technical Writing, Comprehension in Reading, Reading for the 70's? We can furnish an abundance of proof that we are constantly relating to the world "out there," bringing into our classroom the world "out there," and in some cases taking our students "out there" to participate.

We present some examples of *existing* courses:

In a Consumer English class students study banking, borrowing money, setting up a budget, establishing credit, consumer law, and buying or renting a house. They hear speakers from finance companies, credit agencies, and a consumer protection bureau. They visit banks, set up budgets, search newspaper ads for bargains in food, clothing, and furniture.

In a Journalism class students write features, editorials, stories, columns, and advertisements. They solicit advertisements from the community in order to finance their publication. They cover their beats in the city, and they visit a printing plant. They hear speakers from the field of journalism: reporters, editors, columnists, sports writers, and photographers.

In a Mass Media class, students decide to sponsor a lunch-time radio show.
 They write a rationale and proposal, including a description of technical
 equipment and costs, which they present to the Faculty Advisory Council
 for adoption. They gather news, write it up to fit the time slots, run the
 show, and conduct polls to assess listener reaction. In a television project,
 the students write scripts for teaching abstract concepts (including "the
 subordinate clause"). They learn about the use of the equipment and
 strengthen their communitcations skills by producing their program.
In an elective called Community Action Through Reading and English students
 become teacher aides in Head Start programs and elementary and junior high
 school classrooms. They work in a program in a local hospital where they
 read to and talk with children and run a small TESOL program for Spanish
 speakers struggling to master English.
In Community Survey—a social studies-English elective—students accumulate
 data about the school, the relationship between the community and the
 school, the community's view of education, and the needs and resources of
 the school and the community." They interview townspeople, educators,
 civic leaders, and other students; they structure questionnaires and debate
 the validity of the items; they produce and edit a book to record the results
 of the survey and serve as a reference for further school action.

It will not surprise other English teachers, though it may surprise those who
accuse us of teaching "abstract academic subjects which have no meaning and
little purpose," that all but one of these classes were conceived and implemented
before 1970 by teachers who knew nothing of career education and who now
interpret it as another opponent intent on belittling—without understanding—the
efforts of good teachers like themselves.

It will not surprise other English teachers, but it should surprise career educationalists, that in spite of updated objectives, student directed classes, modern-
ized classroom techniques, hard work by the good teacher, more training, and
more resourcefulness, there were students who were bored, who dropped out,
who went untouched. As long as the new content, new techniques, and new
motivation did not require them to work much, did not spill over into their
world of wheels and girls, (or boys), they did not complain.

How do we English teachers meet the challenge of career education? We answer it by knowing what career education is (and is not), by knowing what the
needs of our students are today and tomorrow, by reevaluating our goals, by
refurbishing our classroom strategies, and by continuing our training.

We meet the challenge by advertising our accomplishments and continuing our
improvement. We meet it by rejecting the idea that all school is boring, that
schools are to blame for all the ills of society, and that negative attitudes toward
school will be cured by integrating the world of work into every classroom at
every level.

We meet the challenge by teaching and counseling our students that caring about minority rights, senior citizens, political honesty, and self-knowledge are equally if not more important than earning a living.

We meet it by asking the U.S. Office of Education not to use its concentrated resources to change the structure and goals of American education but to provide funds for easing the struggle that depletes and inhibits the good teacher. But we ask that these notions of what constitutes quality come from English teachers themselves and not from some outside source, no matter what its status or quality. Let those of us who work in the profession have at least a voters privilege in setting its policies and goals.

Finally, in assessing our challenges to career education, we are moved to voice a few challenges of our own. What will be the reaction to a constant diet of career education from K through 12? What evidence has been used to lead the proponents of career education to conclude that elementary children should spend a portion of each day learning about vocations. Even if they do, does it follow that this will cure the ills of school? Of society? The class system? The problems of a technological society? What is the rationale for thinking that the schools can equip students to compete with a trade school graduate or a journeyman? Why do the career advocates believe that integrating the world of work into all courses at all levels will insure good teaching? If career education is the solution to school problems, why aren't existing vocational classes over-subscribed? Will a "vitalized" secondary school curriculum solve such personal problems of young adults as split families, the generation gap, the fight to be independent, the cost of peer acceptance? Is it wise to proclaim that career education will add meaning to even abstract disciplines, will rout boredom, will meet the nation's manpower requirements when the technological world already has its share of dropouts, the apathetic, and the bored?

English taught at its best is meeting the needs of today's young people, for it teaches the skills of language. It is meeting students' needs because it takes them beyond the utilitarian and the material. It is meeting the challenge of skeptics because taught at its best, it helps the schools in achieveing what Commissioner Marland in 1971 said is a prime requisite of today's education: to equip the youngster to live his life as a fulfilled human being. We diverge only on what brings that fulfillment about.

Raymond E. Wanner

EXPANDING ON
CAREER EDUCATION*

The European Ministers of Education, meeting in Bern last June, strongly agreed on three basic recommendations: that young people in making their choice of studies should take into account the employment possibilities that will ultimately be available to them, that academic and vocational-technical education should be more closely coordinated, and that specialization at too early an age should be avoided. It was almost as if the conference reports and resolutions had come from sessions held in Chicago or Atlanta, and that the subject had been "career education."

Behind the Bern discussions lay the fact that in most Western European countries the imperatives of social, technological, and industrial change have made the traditional rigid separation of general or academic education from vocational-technical education a serious pedagogical and social liability. Likewise, greatly increased occupational mobility and the need for constant updating of knowledge and skills have underscored the need for society to view formal education not only in terms of the education of the young but also as a continuing social service available to citizens throughout their lifetime.

As the Ministers of Education met in the Swiss capital, other international bodies met in various locations throughout Europe. More often than not, it seemed, one could detect in their deliberations one or more variations on the theme of career education. In early June, for example, the European Comparative Education Society held its Sixth General Conference in Rome. Its goal was to study and, it was hoped, to refine the Organization for Economic Cooperation and Development's (OECD) concept of recurrent education, one of several strategies proposed in recent years to make the ideal of lifelong education a practical, realizable reality for men and women whose possibilities for continuing education have heretofore been limited by job or other responsibilities.

Later that same month, the OECD itself sponsored a conference on "Future Structures of Postsecondary Education." Participants discussed, among other tings, the relationship of postsecondary education, in both its traditional and evolving patterns, to labor market processes.

The Council of Europe, working mostly through workshops, symposiums, and publications, has also taken an active role in promoting the concept and practice

*Raymond E. Wanner—"Expanding on Career Education" reprinted with permission from the November, 1973 issue of *American Education*.

of career-relative education. It has proposed to its member states new structures and mechanisms on the postsecondary level to upgrade technical education and incorporate it into the comprehensive university system. Efforts in this direction will very likely lead to the creation of more "short cycle" institutions such as the two year French University Institutes of Technology (I.U.Ts).

In Amsterdam, planners at the European Cultural Foundation are nearing completion of the education section of an ambitious project called "Plan Eropa 2000." They will concentrate during the next phase of their research on problems related to education, employment, and the economy.

For its part, the European Community is about to expand its activity in the field of education through its new directorate general for research, science, and education. In its published work plan it cities "the relationship between education and occupation (content of education, structures of demand, career prospects, and the like)" as one of the major problems in European education. With its decision-making powers and economic strength, it is expected that the Community will make a significant contribution to the solution of career-related educational problems.

It is interesting to note also that the theme of the UNESCO-International Bureau of Education's 34th session of the International Conference on Education held in September was "The Relationship Between Education, Training, and Employment with Particular Reference to Secondary Education. Its Aims, Structure, and Content." The background and working papers of this conference represent a truly international cross section of job-related educational practice and insight. Similarly, the UNESCO-sponsored Faure Report, *Learning to Be*, (1972) provides valuable insights into the relationship of education to career in "a learning society."

Finally, at the International Labor Conference, which met in Geneva last June 6–27, the issue of paid educational leave was raised and discussed at some length. This term is understood in the International Labor Office literature to mean time off from normal working hours (as distinct from vacation time with pay for recreational purposes) to give employees "the opportunity and incentive to acquire the further education and training which they need to carry out their duties at the workplace and to assume their responsibilities as members of the community."

As early as 1964 UNESCO invited member countries to consider legislation for such leave. Since then, the Council of Europe and the OECD have also recommended strongly that educators, labor officials, and governments give serious consideration to paid educational leave as part of any strategy of continuing education. Discussion of this topic at the International Labor Conference was in very positive terms.

From such conferences and meetings and from governmental and university research, certain common themes are gradually emerging about the relationship of public education to personal development and gainful employment. There is general agreement, for example, that the quality of vocational-technical education needs to be improved and that its status relative to traditional academic education must be elevated. Many educational planners believe that this will require much closer integration of academic and vocational education programs. Thus, young people who, after extensive guidance and counseling, have chosen to specialize in vocational and technical subjects would nevertheless receive a basic grounding in general and humanistic education. Those whose programs are more specifically academic would, for their part, have a vocational, career-oriented dimension added to their curriculum. For the vocational-technical student, increased exposure to the humanities could conceivably develop a taste for serious literature and the fine arts and open up new possibilities for personal development as well as career flexibility and opportunities for further study. For the student in an academic track, the addition of a vocational-career education dimension to the school experience could well mean the difference between getting or not getting a job in a society that is increasingly demanding of its academic generalists one or more marketable skills.

There is a growing conviction also that education should be available to all citizens over the course of their lifetime and not be considered as the exclusive right of the under-30 generation. Conversely, there is an emerging reluctance to impose education on those who, at least temporarily, are unwilling to receive it. According to this point of view, it makes more sense for a young person only marginally attracted to school to enter the labor market for a period of time and perhaps later return to a formal program of general education. To be workable, it would seem that such a pattern of recurring work and study would have to take place in a social and legislative context that would guarantee employees the right to periodic educational sabbaticals.

Any large scale implementation of educational programs on a basis of recurrent work and study would require also that the time off the job be with pay and normal insurance and other fringe benefits. Thus, the International Labor Office's recent favorable consideration of paid educational leave as a basic right of workers and its likely endorsement of the practice next year is considered by many observers to be of considerable social importance.

Lest the concept of a worker's sabbatical or paid educational leave be banished out of hand to the never-never land of grand but impossible idealistic social schemes, it should be borne in mind that it is, in fact, already a legislative and functional reality in many countries. In principle, at least, it has been supported by 58 of the 60 countries that responded to the ILO questionnaire on the topic. In the United States one should not overlook, as examples of the direction such legislation might take initially, the Government Employees' Training Act and various civil service regulations which "provide for the payment of salaries as compensation to employees undergoing training considered necessary for the performance of their official duties." Of particular note are such current HEW-sponsored programs as Project Stride and the Upward Mobility College, which under certain circumstances allow employees time off the job with pay to pursue their studies. In its most evolved form, paid educational leave would provide all workers the opportunity not only for training directly related to their professional responsibilities, but also for a wide variety of non-job-related study, including what the literature describes as trade union education.

A legislative proposal including these provisions is currently being debated in the Netherlands, where labor unions are negotiating with government officials for a work week for young workers made up of three days on the job and two days of paid educational leave. The case for workers 15 and 16 years old has already been won. Meanwhile the unions continue to argue that since university students are highly subsidized by the government, workers in the age group 17–24 should also have the right to some educational services at government expense. This is especially so, they say, since the workers already are economic producers, contribute to the GNP, and pay taxes. A key point in their proposal is that their educational leave may be used for general and trade union education. A Dutch official said recently that the government is quite sympathetic to the workers' demands and that, at the very least, existing programs of so-called participation education will be expanded in philosophical concept and academic offerings.

Participation education itself is still very much of an experiment in Holland. It has sprung from two forms of education which have existed for some time; namely, the apprenticeship system and the educational institutes for working youths 18 years of age and under. It is usually described as education which consists of a school component and a society or career component which interact to produce a harmonious learning situation. Formal programs of participation education were introduced only in 1970 and it is, perhaps, premature to attempt to evaluate them. Dutch officials are confident, however, that the experience gained in this venture with regard to individualized teaching, the introduction of the career component to general education, and methods of working with groups will undoubtedly be of significant general value to Dutch education regardless of how participation education, as such, is judged in the future.

Switzerland and the Federal Republic of Germany also have a tradition of combining work experience, vocational-technical training, and general education. It is a tradition that undoubtedly contributes to the high quality of industrial workmanship these countries are generally conceded to enjoy.

In Denmark, a 1968 Act on Leisure Time Education and its 1971 amendments provide for paid educational leave to certain categories of workers. There are, similarly, highly developed programs of worker and adult education in Norway and Sweden, and citizens are encouraged to take advantage of them by financial grants, paid leave, and other support granted under stated conditions. Moreover, in Sweden a governmental ruling in 1969 gave access to universities to all those over 25 years of age who have had five years work experience even though they may not have earned the secondary school diplomas normally required for admission.

Such arrangements complement the work of the Nordic folk high school, a Scandinavian institution founded over 100 years ago in Denmark to provide education in civic responsibility to young adults. The schools are coeducational and residential and offer courses that are usually three to ten months in duration. These are generally considered to be on a more general and popular level than university courses. The folk high shcool continues to enjoy considerable success in Scandinavia, and its philosophy and programs are constantly being updated. The forthcoming report of the triannual Nordic folk high meeting held last August will be a valuable source of current thought on folk high school education. It is interesting to contemplate the possibility of an American form of participation education that might combine the folk high school concept with industry-based career education. Under-utilized facilities of military, academic, and religious institutions could, perhaps, be leased to house such an experiment.

American officials may wish also to study the details of the Belgian legislation of April 10, 1973, granting certain workers an amount of extra paid vacation time equal to the number of hours of approved study they followed after working hours. This law, known as *"la loi sur les crédits d' heures,"* represents a significant compromise between management, government, and union interests and could provide a working model for national groups which take the view that if any form of paid educational leave is to be provided at all, it must be introduced very cautiously. Opponents of the Belgian plan argue that many of the workers who are most in need of further general and technical education will not have the motivation to seek it after the fatigue of a full day's work. They suggest that time off the job with pay during regular working hours would respond more fully to workers' needs.

The July 1971 French legislation on vocational, technological, and continuing education is of great importance in that an advanced industrial state, long committed to elitist education, assumed what it specifically called an *"obligation nationale"* to provide the necessary legal and administrative mechanisms for the continuing education of its workers. The law provided, among other things, the right to paid educational leave to workers in enterprises having at least ten employees. The Office of Education's Institute of International Studies published much of the text of this law as well as an introductory interpretation under the title *A French Approach to Career Education* (DHEW Publication No. OE 73-19100).

Educators and social scientists are following the implementation of this law and the development of similar policies of recurrent education and paid educational leave with considerable interest. Some serious thinkers have already pointed out that the very fact that labor unions, employers, government officials, and educators are working together as social partners in several countries to plan finance, and implement these specialized educational programs has, in itself, very positive long-range implications for solving complex social problems.

Recent experience in France and elsewhere in Western Europe suggests also that education on a recurrent or periodic basis has substantial and potentially far-reaching administrative, structural, and pedagogical ramifications for existing educational institutions. How would they, for example, adapt their degree requirements and their admissions, course unit, and transfer credit policies to coordinate a series of periodic academic experiences into a unified program of studies? That these experiences may range over an extended period of time and include anything from micro-mini-courses in several different institutions to year-long programs of full-time study on a university campus considerably compliments traditional academic bookkeeping. More importantly, how will they adapt their teaching to meet the dual challenge of developing fully the human qualities of technological man and bringing the tools of technological progress to humanistic studies?

The ever-increasing diversity of the form and content of contemporary education would seem to demand, furthermore, that some effort be made to establish equivalencies between traditional and nontraditional academic qualifications. It is unlikely that society will soon abandon the concept of credentials, and insofar as academic and other credentials help maintain certain standards of training, this is perhaps not to be regretted. It does seem desirable, however, that a wider variety of skills be recognized as giving the social and economic status traditionally reserved for academic diplomas and that individuals be allowed to sit for examinations granting degree equivalency on the basis of work experience and demonstrated ability. These are, in fact, matters that the Council for National Academic Awards, which since 1964 has awarded degrees to British students completing specified programs of study in nondegree granting institutions, has for some time had under consideration. The Gould Commission on Non-Traditional Study has also made important recommendations in this area.

Just as the social and pedagogical issues raised by the career education concept in the United States appear in fact to have their counterparts in Western Europe, researchers and educators in the United States searching for new approaches to these issues also have their European counterparts. In many cases working relationships and channels for the regular exchange of information already have been established between them. The encouragement and growth of such contacts could bring increased benefits to European and American educators alike. One can hope that by working together they may come upon pedagogical insights which would produce a 20th century version of the *habile et honnête homme*, that ideal citizen whom 17th century educators, faced with their own knowledge explosion and scientific revolution, considered to be grounded enough in the humanities to understand his cultural heritage and skilled enough in the public forum to be an active, useful, and productive member of society.